SO, Where's Your THESIS?

SO, Where's Your THESIS?

Derek Irwin, Ph.D.
University of Nottingham Ningbo China

Viktoria Jovanovic-Krstic, Ph.D.
University of Toronto and
Humber College Institute of Technology and Advanced Learning

Bruce Watson, M.A.
York University and University of Toronto

NELSON / EDUCATION

NELSON / EDUCATION

So, Where's Your Thesis?
by Derek Irwin, Viktoria Jovanovic-Krstic, and Bruce Watson

Vice President, Editorial Higher Education:
Anne Williams

Executive Editor:
Laura Macleod

Marketing Manager:
Amanda Henry

Developmental Editor:
Leah Blain

Permissions Coordinator:
Melody Tolson

Content Production Manager:
Claire Horsnell

Production Service:
Cenveo Publisher Services

Copy Editor:
Heather Sangster, Strong Finish

Proofreader:
GanesanRamalingam

Indexer:
BIM Indexing & Proofreading

Production Coordinator:
Ferial Suleman

Design Director:
Ken Phipps

Managing Designer:
Franca Amore

Interior Design:
Dianna Little

Cover Design:
Dianna Little

Cover Image:
badahos/iStockphoto

Interior Design Image:
badahos/iStockphoto

Compositor:
Cenveo Publisher Services

Printer:
R.R. Donnelley

Library and Archives Canada Cataloguing in Publication

Irwin, Derek, 1972-
So, where's your thesis? / Derek Irwin, Viktoria Jovanovic-Krstic, Robert Bruce Watson.

Includes bibliographical references and index.
ISBN 978-0-17-650445-8

1. English language--Rhetoric.
2. Essay--Authorship. 3. Report writing. I. Jovanovic-Krstic, Viktoria, 1970- II. Watson, Robert Bruce, 1973- III. Title.

PE1471.I79 2012   808'.042
C2011-906389-1

ISBN-13: 978-0-17-650445-8
ISBN-10: 0-17-650445-1

This book is dedicated to my husband, Aleksandar, and my children, Nastasia-Simonida and Lazar, who have waited patiently while I completed revisions and who have given up family time with me in an effort to help me work through the chapters. This book is also dedicated to the students who have, over the years, offered valuable insight into suggested chapters and topics. Finally, this book is dedicated to every person interested in improving their essay writing skills—good luck to you all!

VIKTORIA JOVANOVIC-KRSTIC

I dedicate this book first of all to my wife, Andrea, and my children, Caleb and Tyler. You are my inspiration for life, and I thank you for your forbearance during the many nights that I wrote while you slept. To all my students, and especially to those who let us quote from their work, thank you for all the times you asked, "But, professor, why did I get this grade?" This book is in many ways our best attempt to answer your question, and I hope we got it right. And finally, a "shout-out" to my dear co-authors, Viktoria Jovanovic-Krstic and Derek Irwin: writing this book with you was as fun as teaching grammar together, but I think that students will like this textbook much better!

BRUCE WATSON

This book is dedicated to my wife, Susan, and my children, Georgia and Jamie. These are the ones who have to put up with my late nights and muttering incessantly about monkeys and grammar. I also thank my co-authors, my editors and my students for similar patience!

DEREK IRWIN

TABLE OF CONTENTS

Preface   x

Acknowledgements   xii

CHAPTER 1 Pre-Writing: The Necessary First Step   1

Beginning with the Preliminaries—Thinking
About the Essay and the Topic   2

Writing from a Reading Means Reading First   5

Thinking About the Audience—Writing for Readers   8

Writing with a Plan—The Role of the Outline   9

Collecting Information Appropriately   13

Putting It All Together in an Outline   20

Tying It All Together   29

Notes   29

CHAPTER 2 Introductions and Thesis Statements   31

Introductions   31

Generating Focus and Reader Interest   35

Opening Strategies   36

Thesis Statements   40

Getting From Your Topic to Your Thesis   44

Fixing Thesis Statements   47

The Thesis Is the Doorway to Your Essay   50

Notes   51

CHAPTER 3 Writing Body Paragraphs   53

Beginning at the Beginning: So, What is
a Paragraph?   53

It's All About the Topic Sentence   54

Using Examples Effectively   56

Cohesion and Coherence in Paragraph Structure   58

Developing Paragraphs Logically Through
Definition, Explanation, and Qualification   61

Organizing the Paragraphs   63

Special Consideration: Spicing Up
Your Paragraphs   69

The Concluding Sentence   72

Notes   73

CHAPTER 4   So, What Is My Thesis?: Creating a
Valid and Valuable Argument   **75**

How to Approach a Topic Critically   75

Different Approaches to Argument   76

Applying Objective Analysis to Answer the
Question "What does my professor
want *me* to do?"   80

Errors in Argument: An Examination of
Common Logical Fallacies   82

Notes   89

CHAPTER 5   Organizing the Discussion:
The "Thinking Body" of Your Essay   **91**

The Big Picture: Using Organization
to Make Your Point   91

Consider a Traditional Approach   92

How to Organize Your Paper Around
an Argument   95

Organizing Your Paper Around Your Argument   104

Bringing It All Together: Using the
Toulmin Model to Organize Your Papers   107

Using Research as an Organizing Device   109

The Mechanics of Citation: MLA,
APA, and CMS Styles   110

The Relevance of Researched Material   112

Integration   113

Order   114

Some Final Points   115

Notes   116

CHAPTER 6   **Concluding with Finesse**   **117**

Having the Last Word   117

How Not to Conclude an Essay   118

The Key Elements of Successful Conclusions   120

Driving Your Point Home: Giving Your Reader Something to Keep Thinking About   122

Conclusion to the Conclusion   125

CHAPTER 7   **The Role of Revision in the Writing Process**   **127**

What to Consider During the Revision Process   128

Revision as the Means of Eliminating "Clutter"   130

Reapproaching Adverbs and Adjectives   131

A Note on Rhetorical Devices and Revision   133

Notes   135

CHAPTER 8   **Understanding the Grammar of Writing**   **137**

The Basic Problem   137

Combining Clauses: Coordination and Subordination   142

Grammatically Correct but Poor Form   146

The Clause as Message   152

Note   154

CHAPTER 9   Tying It All Together   **155**

The Imitation Journal Explained   156

Appendix A   How Essays Are Marked   **159**

Appendix B   More on Citation   **167**

Index   **183**

PREFACE

A NOTE FROM THE AUTHORS

The idea for *So, Where's Your Thesis?* began in 2006 when a keen young student in one of our classes kept on writing and kept on receiving a less than perfect grade without fully understanding why. In fact, this particular student argued quite adamantly that he had spent more than 10 hours on a particular paper and so thought he deserved much better than a C. While diligence is certainly a hallmark of all the A+ students we have ever known, alas, successful essay writing depends on far more than the amount of time spent on a paper. One day after receiving his third straight C, the young man went to visit Bruce. Quite upset and growing more exasperated by the minute, he waved his paper and exclaimed, "Why did I get a C? I followed the instructions and I did the research, so why aren't you giving me an A?" Bruce took the paper, skimmed it very quickly, and replied, "So, where's your thesis? With no thesis, your paper lacks a discernible purpose: you need to tell us your hypothesis—what your essay will attempt to do—so that we can follow *how* you reach your conclusions. Without a thesis to guide your readers, they have no idea why they're reading your paper."

Where we teach, as in most universities, A+ is that elusive "perfect" grade the young man was seeking—the highest grade that any instructor can give a paper and the implicit standard against which all papers are judged. But what is an A+ paper? And how do we know the difference between an A+ and an A or, for that matter, between an A and a C? That question is both totally legitimate and completely relevant to your academic success, and this book is your best answer. Though there are hundreds of other books telling you how you should write essays, only *So, Where's Your Thesis?* approaches the topic of writing through the issue of your grades. We do so because you probably care somewhat more about your grades than about becoming a better essayist, but also because we believe that understanding how your papers are evaluated will help you write better essays.

This guide is unique in that it provides a glimpse into the mind of the marker: your "prof." Our combined years of experience on both sides of the evaluation game have convinced us that explaining our expectations in terms of grades helps our students improve their writing rapidly. As students, we came to write A+ papers by learning to meet and exceed our markers' expectations, and as professors, we have taught students to succeed at the academic essay by understanding how their work is evaluated. The path to better writing involves more than hard work alone, but there are some shortcuts to success, and this book is packed with tips that are all correlated to specific marking criteria.

We also provide a sample generic marking scheme to help you understand how your mark results from your performance against specific criteria such as organization and argument. Disclosing and explaining this marking scheme will, we hope, have several effects. First, you will understand more clearly what an A+ is when you see how it results from consistent excellence across all of the marking criteria. Second, from that understanding, you may choose to shoot for the A+ by working on everything at once or to work on one skill at a time. Either way, you will see results.

We hope that you sincerely enjoy this book by accepting it in the manner with which it is intended. This is not a be-all, end-all book on essay writing, but it is our sincere attempt to take the paralyzing fear out of writing academic essays. While our approach to essay writing is based on understanding your professors' expectations, we hope that you find that every chapter teaches specific skills that make you a better, and more successful, essay writer. We are confident that *So, Where's Your Thesis?* will not only have an immediate impact on your writing but will continue to improve your writing throughout your university or college career.

Also, if you give it a chance, you might begin to think that writing is a bit of fun.

ACKNOWLEDGEMENTS

We wrote this book for you, the student, because learning to write good essays was one of the most difficult things we ever did. The learning was hard, and it took years, so we remember it all very clearly: the disappointing grades, the poring over barely legible comments to find out where we had gone wrong, the thousands of lectures and books we absorbed, the writing exercises we did, the grammar books we studied, and, most of all, the joy at seeing the proof of our progress as our grades improved.

There are so many people without whom this book could never have been written. First in line are our spouses, Aleksandar, Susan, and Andrea, who suffered many lonely nights while we marked papers, prepared lectures, then wrote until sunrise. Without your long-suffering support, love, and understanding, this book would still be no more than a great idea for a book.

We also want to thank the entire Nelson Education team, beginning with Laura Macleod and Leah Blain, whose energy and direction rocketed us through the revision stage and really helped make this a far clearer and more helpful book on essay writing. Our very special thanks go out to all the reviewers for their many insights and valuable feedback. They include Stephen Ahern (Acadia University), Trevor Arkell (Humber College), Greg Doran (University of PEI), Rob Falconer (Grant MacEwan University), Chandra Hodgson (Humber College), Karen Inglis (Kwantlen Polytechnic University), Krista Kesselring (Dalhousie University), Christine Kirchner (Camosun College), and Jillian Skeffington (Grant MacEwan University). We owe a debt of gratitude to Heather Sangster at Strong Finish and her laser-eye copy-editing for catching all those "typographical malfunctions" and all those explanations and attempts at humour that probably wouldn't have made sense to 90 percent of our readers.

And finally, we want to thank all our students: Jane and Julie in particular for letting us quote from your essays, but also the hundreds of students we have taught over the past decade. Ultimately, your learning experiences in our classrooms were our inspiration; your successes taught us which teaching approaches work, and every single one of your struggles changed how we taught in the future and shaped our approach to every topic in this book. Without all of you, this book could never have been written.

Derek Irwin, University of Nottingham Ningbo China

Viktoria Jovanovic-Krstic, University of Toronto and Humber College Institute of Technology and Advanced Learning

Bruce Watson, York University and University of Toronto

Pre-Writing:

The Necessary First Step

The first thing to make peace with is that pre-writing is *not optional*. Pre-writing is an essential step in the writing process. Students who pre-write effectively do see better results in the finished product; in fact, students who pre-write have a more enjoyable writing process, period. And, although it is true that the pre-writing process does not always get you to the conclusion any faster, it does do other very important things:

- It helps you discover what you want to write about.

- It forces you to read critically and analytically.

- It encourages you to come up with a focus for your paper.

- It enables you to break up your paper into its working parts—its topics and arguments—so you can begin strategizing about how you will put them all together.

- It helps you map out a game plan.

- It allows you to envision how the structure of your work will evolve.

- It shifts the task of writing from the most difficult part (squaring off against that blank page) to the easiest (mapping with an outline), a shift some writing instructors call "front-ending."

So why else would you pre-write if the reasons above were not enough? Well, the pre-writing process is also the collection and examination process. During the pre-writing stage, many fundamental decisions take place—decisions that require you to consider not only what you are writing about, but also whom you are writing for and how you intend to clarify your focus. And if those reasons are not enough, pre-writing enables you to write better papers more quickly by forcing you to narrow your purpose and come up with a plan. In other words, becoming a more efficient writer will help you do better in all your courses by meeting deadlines and having more time for editing and revision.

BEGINNING WITH THE PRELIMINARIES— THINKING ABOUT THE ESSAY AND THE TOPIC

There are many ways to begin thinking about your essay, and for the most part, no one pre-writing exercise is better than another, although certain exercises work better at certain stages of the pre-writing process. This chapter is not about telling you how to create box diagrams and circle charts to get your creative juices flowing; those exercises are useful when you are trying to think of something to write about but don't tell you how to turn those topics into an essay. This chapter will walk you through how you might start considering the writing process. It begins with some questions to ask yourself, discusses the critical steps you should follow, and then helps you come up with a habitual process to run through every time you prepare to write an essay. Simply having a process to go through will prevent hours of staring at a blank screen—and by moving you from having nothing to having something, pre-writing virtually eliminates the type of stress that can paralyze you for days at square one of the writing process.

To make the pre-writing process seem far less arduous and much more applicable, this chapter will consider the options that many students have, namely, writing from a reading or writing on a free topic with few or no constraints. It will, therefore, consider in some detail the resources available during this first critical stage—resources such as the Internet, the library, or the reading that students may need to base their paper on. These resources are invaluable sources for potential essay topics when the essay topic is not supplied.

So let us begin.

Understanding the Essay and the Task at Hand

The instructions for an academic essay usually fall into three major groups.

1. Students are given a choice from a number of options and asked to pick one.

2. Students are given very broad choices and asked to narrow down the topics into something that is workable.

3. Students are given very broad parameters, such as "write an argumentative or analytical essay, eight to ten pages in length."

Whatever the circumstances, the first and most important aspect of the pre-writing process is to understand the terminology of the assignment itself. That is, *you need to understand and do only what is required.* Although this task may sound simple, one of the most common errors in undergraduate academic writing is failure to comply with the confines of the assignment. Especially in first-year papers, not answering the question is responsible for many C, D, and F papers; those essays miss the point, get only half of the point, or attempt to do far more than the assignment intended. Understanding the initial question is an important aspect of the pre-writing process because so much of your grade lies in your ability to discern what your professor wants you to do, and why. Many a student has submitted an excellently written paper on a topic that has little or nothing to do with the original topic. Such a paper, rather than receiving a grade of A+, usually receives a lacklustre C. You must understand your topic before you can do any better.

So how can you understand a topic? There are a number of set questions you can ask yourself to help you make sense of your topic and your intended audience and to help you begin thinking about the assignment in the right frame of mind. For instance:

- Do I really understand all the key terms in the essay assignment?

- Am I being asked to *analyze* (examine the structure of something critically; consider how some structure or aspect of a thing or a text works); to *argue* (prove or adopt a position and defend it, for example); to *examine* (explore or consider the significance or value of some idea, point, or phenomenon and to subsequently examine its strengths and weaknesses, perhaps providing some interpretative commentary); to *compare* or *contrast*; or to *define the causes* or *effects* of some phenomenon? The format of your paper will ultimately depend on the key terms of the essay question itself, so you must become intimately familiar with them.

- Does the assignment ask me to do *more than one thing*? Am I expected to analyze and argue? If so, are the requirements of my assignment prioritized?

- What do I already know about the topic I am being asked to write about?

- Do I have a specific direction or focus in mind, or will I have to spend some time *thinking* about this and researching it?

- How many pages am I required to write? Remember, the word or page limit is an incredibly important part of the planning process because detail is very important in academic essays. Your professors use the page or word limit to indicate the scope of your argument and the level of detail you are expected to provide, and you will ignore their instructions at your peril.

- Am I expected to use secondary sources, such as book-length studies or essays from peer-reviewed journals? If so, are these secondary sources intended as supplementary materials or is my assignment to be based entirely on primary research?

Once you understand the requirements of the essay assignment, then you can begin the second critical aspect of pre-writing: narrowing a general topic down to a workable academic idea that can be supported coherently and cohesively in a set number of pages. Since most academic essays ask you to take either an analytical or argumentative approach, and since many essays are based on an assigned reading, we will now discuss how to write an essay based on a reading. We will look first at how to approach both the analytical and the argumentative essay from the perspective of reading and writing as processes that are essentially intimate acts.

WRITING FROM A READING MEANS READING FIRST

Let's imagine that the essay is the traditional eight- to ten-page paper on an assigned reading or other work. This may be literary or non-fiction prose, an article from a newspaper or

---

GRAMMAR **TIP**

Dashes (—) are longer than hyphens (-). Dashes are used— sparingly!—to offset text in a clause. If you remove the dashed text, the sentence should still make sense. Hyphens are used for compound description words acting together before a noun, such as "high-class monkey" or "bare-bones bar," and for spelled-out fractions, such as "one-fifth." Hyphens are also used for some common compound nouns, such as "X-ray" or "sister-in-law." But there is no real consistency to which ones take a hyphen, so check your dictionary!

---

professional journal, a Web page, or a film. Whatever the genre, there are several easy steps that will help you select a clear and concise essay topic that fulfills the requirements of your assignment and—most importantly—connects your essay topic to the reading in an analytical and academic fashion. And if you aspire to a good grade on your paper, you must begin by reading very, very closely.

Teasing Out a Possible Topic: The "So what?" and "Seems to be about" Models[1]

Sometimes the biggest problem is not with understanding the rubrics of the assignment, but rather with approaching the text critically, analytically, and argumentatively. Critical reading and thinking leads to critical writing. Approaching a reading critically and analytically requires that you approach a text not from a comprehensive perspective—"I understand"—but rather from an analytical and critical perspective—"I interpret this to mean," or, in the words of Rosenwasser and Stephen (56), "This seems to be about X." Simply put, reading analytically means examining everything in a text *as if there were a double agenda*. It means asking, "So what?" after you have considered what an original proposition or statement *seems to be about*. If you think, "I like this article because of its provocative subject matter," ask yourself, "What is provocative? What do I mean by the word *provocative*? How would I explain the idea of provocative to someone? What examples in this essay illustrate the word *provocative*? What examples in this essay show that something is provocative?" If you think that a reading is interesting, ask yourself, "Why is this reading interesting? What has captured my interest?" Make a list that begins to isolate what you personally mean by "interesting." This list may be long, and it may even stem off into many directions, but that's okay. Interesting thought processes usually take interesting turns.

If we begin the critical reading process by assuming that all words on the page are relevant, then beginning the interpretative process requires that we understand what something *seems to be about*. It also requires that we ask the right questions.

As you read, ask yourself:

- What is the most interesting sentence in this paragraph? What is the most interesting paragraph on this page? *Why do I think that this information is interesting?*

- What is the most effective example that the writer uses to support an idea? How do I know that an example is effective? How have I interpreted the term *effective*? *Is effectiveness something that I can measure or feel? If so, how?*

- What is the most appropriate example that the writer uses to make a point? How do I know that this is an appropriate example? Do I understand what is meant by the term *appropriate*? *If not, figure it out! Don't assume that just because you're fuzzy on something means it probably isn't important.*

What should be becoming very obvious right now is that the pre-writing process is really as much about reading analytically and critically as it is about writing and brainstorming. In fact, reading and writing are so intimately connected that in order to write well, you must first read carefully.

Since academic essays require more than showing your professor that you understand your subject matter, it is important to examine all readings analytically to see if you can tease out the hidden nuances behind the obvious claims. These hidden claims or assumptions may provide you with just that leverage to approach your essay in an innovative manner. Asking, "Why does it matter?"—or "So what?"—really means that you are considering analytically and critically whether there may be some interesting implications behind the words on the page.

Ask yourself:

- Is there an authorial message hidden between the lines?

- Are the ideals of the time embedded in the diction (word choice)?

- Does the writer of the text use rhetoric in a particular way to prod you toward any conclusions?

- Are there patterns or themes that jump out at you? Do you see any that may be hidden behind certain illustrations or rhetorical devices that the writer uses to make a point?

Since there is never only one possible interpretation to any text, this method can help you to uncover a number of possibilities and at the same time collect the data you need for your essay.

THINKING ABOUT THE AUDIENCE— WRITING FOR READERS

The audience for any essay is the potential reader of that essay. In most of your academic environments, there will be only one potential audience member: your professor. However, based on the type of assignment, your "audience" will expect you to address him or her as a representative of a much broader academic audience. Depending upon your topic and the assignment, that broader audience could be as wide as "any reasonably well-educated and well-informed person" or as narrow as "all specialists in the field of your topic." Needless to say, then, your audience is the most important consideration to take into account early on because the intended audience determines not only how the essay should shape itself, but also why it should do so in a specific way. A thorough audience analysis allows a writer to determine exactly how much information to provide the reader and how to provide this information effectively and appropriately. As you work through your pre-writing exercises, ask yourself:

- Who is my audience? For whom am I writing?

- How much does my audience already know about my subject matter?

- How many examples should I provide to make my point concretely?

- What level of diction (formal or informal) should I use to illustrate my points and present my positions?

- What tone is appropriate for my audience and what type of mood is expected, anticipated, or acceptable?

- Will my audience appreciate some humour, sarcasm, or satire?

- What point of view should I be aiming to express—subjective or objective—and is there a possibility that my choice will affect my grade?

Paying attention to your reader's needs and expectation is an integral step toward writing a solid essay.

WRITING WITH A PLAN—THE ROLE OF THE OUTLINE

Without a doubt, the biggest mistake many students make is to write without a plan. A plan is a necessary aspect of almost anything we do, so why would we write without one? Planning, sometimes known as "outlining," may seem too big of a task for students looking to cut corners but still get an A. The fact of the matter remains, however, that as with most things in life, taking shortcuts only appears to save us some time; something usually goes wrong, and we often spend more time trying to repair the damage than if we had not taken the shortcut to begin with.

Research shows, however, that good writing always begins with some kind of plan,[2] and so this section is all about creating that plan, by first deciding what you will write about and then deciding on an outline that will help you achieve that goal. In the interim, we'll discuss the very important issue of attributing information, and we'll provide you with a fair warning on the topic of plagiarism, which we stress is not something that we take lightly!

Before discussing the outline directly, we need to get through some important first steps: collecting notes and creating a purpose statement. Outlines can only really work when we have a focused topic and when we have some idea of what we want to say about it.

Beginning at the Beginning—Writing the Purpose Statement, or Answering the Question "Why am I writing?"

Choosing what to write about is the most important choice that you can, and must, make. This choice will ultimately determine the scope of your essay and the development of the paper itself.

So, how do we begin? The first thing that you should ask yourself is "Why am I writing?" Even if the answer is "Because my professor is making me," the question should not be avoided. The second question, then, is "What are my choices?" By choices, we mean, what are the criteria you are working within? Do you have a specific topic that you have been assigned? How many words can you devote to the paper itself (what is the page count)? Do you have to use secondary sources? If so, how many? All these questions will contribute to the development of your *working thesis* statement. We use the term *working thesis* because this version will function as a thesis statement and as a road map, all in one. It's like a mini-outline in one sentence. We call this type of thesis statement a purpose statement, and although it is often reserved for academic research papers, it works very nicely in the pre-writing stage of an academic essay.

Writing the Purpose Statement

Here's the concept: it's *very* difficult to think up a perfectly functioning thesis statement with a clearly defined claim out of thin air, then draft an outline, then write a perfectly argued paper, just like that. So instead, once you have used various brainstorming tactics to identify your topics and areas of interest (what you *know* about the problem you're interested in), you then simply try to articulate what you want to *do* (discuss, argue, analyze, etc.), and then identify the topics you think you will need to examine.

For example, if it helps you, begin by expressing this to *yourself*:

> I want to understand how the "one-size-fits-all" work policy of Ontario Works affects single mothers on welfare in Ontario, and to do that, I'll need to carefully research how their policies may reflect social stigmas associated with welfare "deviancy" and "good" motherhood.

Once you have that, presto—you have your purpose statement! To reduce it to a formula, a purpose statement is your *essay topic* (expressed as something you want to *do* with it) + whatever *sub-topics* you will need to examine to accomplish that purpose.

Now, here's the definition: The purpose statement is a statement that outlines very clearly, using vivid verbs, what you intend to do and how you intend to do it. The purpose statement may even begin with the phrase, "The purpose of this paper is to…" You may find a better way to make it 100 percent obvious that this sentence is, in fact, your purpose statement; if you can do so, then good for you!

- The first part of a purpose statement is a stand-in thesis statement that allows you to start writing.

- The second part of a purpose statement is a rough outline for your paper.

- Together, they evolve into a thesis statement and a full outline, then a finished paper.

Whatever way your sentence signals that it is your working thesis, it must (1) specify the purpose of the whole paper and (2) declare how you intend to execute the task. Verbs such as describe, illustrate, examine, criticize, or analyze are often included in the purpose statement, as well as in the focal points of the paper itself. These are the three or so points that the writer tends to elaborate on in an attempt to prove the thesis.

Here is an example of a typical purpose statement:

> The purpose of this paper is to illustrate the importance of pre-writing to the undergraduate Humanities and Social Sciences student. To do this, the paper will aim to discuss the relevance of pre-writing by focusing first on the role of critical and analytical reading, then on the importance of creating a tentative thesis statement, and finally on the necessity of careful outlining. Pre-writing is a necessary aspect of the writing process; students who fail to pre-write jeopardize their chances of attaining an A.

Many students have remarked over the years that purpose statements can seem drawn out and even unsophisticated. In fact, some have said purpose statements don't even seem particularly academic or professional because of their detail. Well, although purpose statements do tend to be quite drawn out, there are some good reasons why you should have one. Essentially, the purpose statement is so specific because it requires that you plan out a course of action before the essay writing process actually begins. Many writers, in fact, use the purpose statement as a type of outline: they print it out and place it somewhere nearby. Then, as they write, they glance from time to time at that statement, using it as map that keeps them on track. The purpose statement, whatever its limitations in creativity, is still the single most important pre-writing tool that a writer can employ. Once you can fully consider both the focus of your paper and how you will realize that focus, you will have taken the first step toward achieving an A, and doing so consistently.

GRAMMAR **TIP**

A lot is two words.

COLLECTING INFORMATION APPROPRIATELY

The first thing we must do before beginning our discussion on how to collect and record information appropriately is to issue our warning on the perils of plagiarism. You need to know what it is and how to avoid getting into serious trouble.

The Perils of the Big P—Plagiarism

Plagiarism is simply the act of passing someone else's ideas or words off as your own, and all too often, plagiarism is the bane of a student's existence. Even though most students have some understanding of what plagiarism is, too many are caught doing it each year. The basic problem with cheating is that it devalues the entire educational experience. If you can receive a degree from my institution without doing the work for it, then everyone's degree is worth that much less. Further, if an institution is graduating people into society who don't actually have the education that they are being given credit for, their lack of competence can have all sorts of undesirable effects. Think about it: do you really want to be treated by a dentist who cheated on exams or live in a building designed by engineers who paid other people to do their assignments? No, none of us want that, so we must accept that the stringent rules governing all kinds of plagiarism exist for our protection.

It is not only ethically important to recognize and acknowledge secondary sources in an essay, but also practically because failing to do so is punishable by failure or even expulsion. In fact, universities spend a great deal of time and effort training faculty how to recognize plagiarism and teaching students how to avoid it. So when it happens, the punishment is often severe. And, although most students monitor their own writing for fear of expulsion, plagiarism continues to be the number-one offence in academic institutions—an offence greatly complicated with the advent of online sources.

The questions that we now must consider are:

- How do we define plagiarism?

- What is the difference between acknowledging information that belongs to someone else and information that is simply common knowledge?

- What is unintentional plagiarism, and is there really such a thing?

- How can we prevent plagiarism?

Defining Plagiarism

As we said above, plagiarism is the representation of another person's or group of people's work as your own. Plagiarism is plagiarism, whether it is one sentence that has been passed off, or an entire paragraph, or an entire paper. Saying, "I forgot to put in a citation" is no excuse either, as plagiarism is still plagiarism even if it's unintentional. Since plagiarism is considered a form of theft by the entire academic community, it is important to differentiate between intentional and unintentional plagiarism and then to examine ways in which to avoid the problem of plagiarism altogether. Heckman's (24–26) succinct guide lays out the fundamentals.*

Intentional plagiarism is:

- Presenting any information that you have taken from another person or text as your own without acknowledging it correctly. This category is broad and includes not only the use of one line (from a poem, book, article, newspaper, essay, etc.), but also entire paragraphs from another work.

- Using information from an online source (including a chat group, discussion group, published documents, or blogs) without putting it in quotation marks and without acknowledging the author of the original work.

- Buying an essay and passing it off as your own.

- Using an essay or information from an essay that you have written for another class and passing it off as original research for this class. This type of plagiarism involves presenting something as an original piece of work when it isn't. But if you think your ideas from another class will benefit you in your essay, you can still use them if you reference them clearly and acknowledge the original source (your original essay).

---

*From HECKMAN. *The Thomson Nelson Guide to Essay Writing*, 2E. © 2007 Nelson Education Ltd. Reproduced by permission. www.cengage.com/permissions.

- Using data (such as quotations, statistics, numbers, percentages, etc.) from a source but failing to provide a point of reference and or an acknowledgement of the source.

- Changing a few words around and shuffling some sentences and then passing information off as your own. The mere substitution of *big* for *large*, for example, may change how a sentence looks, but plagiarism is more than failing to acknowledge the shuffling of words. By shuffling words around and changing them slightly, you have made a great effort to maintain the *original idea* of the piece and to pass it off as your own. Always acknowledge information that comes from another source, even if you have made minor alterations to the original piece.

Unintentional plagiarism is:

- Sloppy documentation or failing to attribute a quote to a source even if you have included quotation marks.

- Sloppy referencing in the body of an essay: even if material has been paraphrased, you must still acknowledge the original source.

BOX 1.2   PLAGIARISM: A CAUTIONARY TALE

I once caught a student plagiarizing a paper. Apparently, in a tremendous hurry, he had found a process-oriented essay online and decided to change the type of process from "Learning How to Swim" to "Learning How to Drive." This cunning plan went awry when I wondered why he had been dreading driving since he was a small child, and how he could learn it by being thrown into a car. I found the original essay online and called the student in to explain why he would be getting a zero on it.

When he sat down in my office, I placed his paper in front of him, along with the online source for it. I pointed out that the bulk of the work was not really his, and so he could not receive credit for the assignment.

He looked at me in amazement and blurted out, "But, professor, I didn't plagiarize—my brother wrote this paper for me!"

Instead of getting a zero on the assignment, this student received a zero in the course.

- Sloppy bibliographic reference of paraphrased material or quoted material.

Drawing the Line between Common Knowledge and Learned Information

The question that now remains is "How do we draw the line between common knowledge and an idea that we originally got from someone else but developed further on our own?" The answer is quite simple: when in doubt, acknowledge! This is as easy as saying: "*According to Heckman (2007), there are many ways to differentiate between intentional and unintentional plagiarism, and they have been illustrated above.*" The dilemma with common knowledge is also quite simple to solve: if you had an idea before you hit the books or the Internet, then that idea is your own. However, once you begin to gather information to develop your idea further, you must attribute and acknowledge accordingly. Ultimately, using the work of others in your own essays shows that you have made an effort to consider other scholars' points of, and it also proves that your essay has a solid foundation in academic thought. Attributing the work of others only makes your ideas stronger.

We will not discuss the mechanics of "doing it right" here, but for those of you with a keen interest, Chapter 5, "Using Research as an Organizing Device," lays it out rather nicely. You might also want to visit the Formatting and Style Guide at the online writing lab (OWL) at Purdue University, West Lafayette, Indiana (http://owl.english.purdue.edu/owl/resources/),[3] for a comprehensive, accessible guide to correct documentation style. Finally, we urge you to visit Appendix B in this book for a succinct discussion and accessible and appropriate examples to help you intentionally or unintentionally find your way around both American Psychological Association (APA) and Modern Language Association (MLA) documentation style.

Doing It Right—Writing Tips to Keep in Mind

Most students say that if and when they plagiarize, it is never intentional; rather, it is a mistake that happened because of poor working habits. We argue that although this is hardly ever the case, it's best for professors not to argue with the student about how the plagiarism happened but to discuss how better habits, such as a better note-taking system or a final revision looking only at sources, might have prevented the act altogether. So here are our favourite tips—tried and true and actually very useful:

At the library

- Always visit the library with the proper tools: pen and paper or laptop. If you can't record sources while you research, you may later become confused about what you read and what you came up with yourself. Particularly, if something sounds good, but you can't recall exactly where it came from, you may be tempted to use the idea without properly citing it. Note, too, that most search engines offered by most libraries' "cyber-library" provide you with a number of very accessible options: RefWorks (which usually requires a login number that can be easily obtained by visiting your institution's reference desk); email options (which usually allow you to email entire texts and/or abstracts to a personal account); folder or search save options (which allow you to save your work in a folder or a separate file using your institution's library system).

- For each secondary source you consult, set aside one to two pages of your notepad. If you use large index cards when researching (they are easy to store and make reusing research easier), be sure to sort your cards by source (using paper clips or rubber bands helps) and record the full citation or call number on every card.

- Clearly mark at the top of each page (or at least on the first index card) the full bibliographic information. Use the following order to help you keep your information clear and correct for future use:

  o **Author.** Write the surname of the author(s), then a comma, then the given name of the author(s) and then a period, e.g., Johnson, Alan.

  o **Title.** Write the full name of the text and edition you are using. Underline the full name of the text. Place a period after the title, e.g., <u>Writing with Ease</u>.

- o **Publication details.** Begin with the place of publication and then add a colon. Write the name of publishing company, followed by a comma and the year of publication, followed by a period, e.g., New York: Pearson, 2009. The finished product should look something like this: Johnson, Alan. <u>Writing with Ease</u>. New York: Pearson, 2009.

- As you take notes, pay special attention to what you are writing down. If you are transcribing word for word, make sure that you enclose those comments in quotation marks. Make sure that all of your quoted material has a referenced page number, even if that information is in the form of a paraphrase or a summary.

- If you are simply jotting down information in point form and summarizing or interpreting the information manually as you go, carefully separate that information from information that is directly quoted. Researchers usually develop a system for safely categorizing different kinds of information: some people use dashes, all caps, or colour codes, but what's crucial is that you come up with an infallible method that shows the difference between what's yours and what's not.

- If you are taking notes from a secondary source that itself is taking notes from another source, note this. Write something to the effect of: "Johnson quoting Firn (26) says …" It is important to differentiate where the information originally comes from and to attribute ideas to the correct source! After all, if you came up with a great idea, you would want the credit to go to you, and not just to the people who quoted you.

- Remember to note *all* the secondary sources that you have used—not just the ones you *think* you are going to use. Sometimes, if you know that you will be referring to a large body of work from one source, it is wise to photocopy those pages directly. Always remember to write down all the reference information on the first page of your photocopied text. For instance: Brindle, Reginald Smith. "The Search Outwards: The Orient, Jazz, Archaisms." <u>The New Music: The Avant-Garde since 1945</u>. New York: Oxford University Press, 1975. 133–45. If you are careful about doing this and about citing every source properly when you use it in the text, you will greatly reduce the likelihood of accidental plagiarism.

Here are some tips on borrowing wisely from online sources:

- With the ease of copying and pasting documents from one source to another, the risk of plagiarism, and particularly accidental plagiarism, becomes much greater. But of course, most writers can clearly tell the difference between their own writing style and the style of the secondary source, so there is no excuse for plagiarism.

- Immediately after you have pasted an online source into your document, highlight that quote, perhaps in another colour or font to separate it. Do not fix the formatting until you have cited it properly.

- Make sure that you have provided the name of the online document/site/Web page and the name of the author(s) if provided. If no author is provided, write *anonymous author* next to the quote or provide the name of the general website as your point of reference.

- Provide the URL and note the date that you retrieved the information.

- Remember that it is your responsibility to document your secondary sources responsibly. Your professor will accept no excuse for not doing so, and in all cases the punishment is not worth the crime.

At the end of the day, keep in mind

Here's the thing. If you haven't noticed, we academics are very weird. We get excited when we see a page full of meticulous citations. Seeing the name of someone we know in print (and especially seeing our own names) makes us feel validated as the book-loving introverts we have dedicated our lives to being. You

WRITING TIP

When in doubt: cite it!

may think that a page full of references doesn't read very well, but most academics agree that you sound smarter when you use their ideas, *if and only if you give them the credit.*

PUTTING IT ALL TOGETHER IN AN OUTLINE

Now that you have collected all kinds of information, the next step is your outline. Unfortunately, many students fail to create an outline and opt rather to move immediately to the writing stage. Not only do those students run the risk of redundant repetition and weak examples, but they also risk poor structure and haphazard arguments. Outlines come in various forms, and the type you choose will depend to a great degree on how well you know your craft and your subject matter. We'll focus our attention on the formal outline, but we'll mention the merits of the scratch outline as we go.

Creating the Outline—From Scratch to Formal

Effective outlines are detailed and they help you see the bones of your ideas; they also make spotting catastrophic errors, such as introducing material not relevant to your topic, easier to see and rectify. Outlines also make the writing process smoother and less stressful, because when you have your ideas clearly marked down, the writing process becomes an exercise of style and refinement rather than a haphazard building up of material.

Scratching Out an Outline

The scratch outline is exactly what its name implies—an outline in less than formal style; one that has as its sole intent the function of providing the writer with a rough guideline. Scratch outlines can be very useful, particularly in the beginning stages of the writing process. Often, students use scratch outlines as a way of quickly organizing their ideas—of getting words on paper before they attempt a larger, more substantial outline. Scratching out an outline is an excellent way to begin thinking about the body of your essay; it is a formidable way of brainstorming possible topics and subtopics and looking for relevant examples. Scratching also leads itself very naturally to the next step—a bona fide formal outline.

Using Sentences to Create a Formal Outline

There are essentially two types of formal outlines that a student can create: topic outlines and sentence outlines. The main differences between them are of detail and time.

Topic outlines show paragraph topics in the order that you intend them to appear in your essay. Topic outlines are developed through the use of key issues or terms that highlight the focus of paragraphs. Topic outlines, because they are more formal and detailed than scratch outlines, work very well for most short essays, especially when you already have a very good idea of what you want to say.

Sentence outlines are the most useful and common outlines for longer, more complex essays. Sentence outlines, like topic

---

GRAMMAR **TIP**

Stuff that can be counted takes the adjective *fewer*, not *less*: "There are fewer and fewer monkeys studying less and less grammar."

---

outlines, break down the structure and format of the essay, but they do so using full sentences instead of single words or short phrases. Sentences outlines are developed using a number of sentences presented in parallel form; they give the writer a clear indication of what he wants to do. They also let a writer see exactly how well developed his ideas are. Further, because sentence outlines use full sentences, the writers tends to see how well developed her examples are and how useful those examples might be to support a topic sentence (in a paragraph, for example) and the thesis statement as a whole.

While both topic outlines and sentence outlines allow you to picture your overall organization by arranging your topics in the correct order, only sentence outlines allow you to figure out *what you will say about those topics*. In fact, they force you to do so. Consider the following two rough outlines that map out the introduction of a real first-year A+ paper: both outlines represent a stage of development before the formal outline, and both follow the same thesis statement. See for yourself which one would help you write a better paper.

Thesis statement: "While student depression can take root in academic stress, it also originates from ineffectively mediated interpersonal relationships and disturbed eating behaviours."*

First, the topical outline:

- depression

- research

- relational problems and depression

- altered eating habits

And now the sentence outline:

- "Depression takes many forms and varies in severity, from temporarily decreased motivation and concentration to severe chronic dejection."

- "Thus far, most research has tended to treat relational problems and disturbed diet as separate bases of depression."

*Student Paper used with permission. Student writer: Jane Yinuo Yao. "Altered Diet: An Adverse Mediator between Interpersonal Problems and Depression in University Students."

- "It is important to note that ineffectively managed relational problems and depression do not simply relate to one another by a one-way causal association, but they take part in a self-enforcing cycle of depression like a positive feedback loop."

- "Bearing in mind that people with relational problems also embody disturbed diet to cope with their issues and that disturbed diet itself is highly correlated with depression, this survey study hypothesizes that altered eating habits, too, mediate the feedback loop."

These examples should demonstrate three advantages of the sentence outline. The first is that there is a big difference between having a topic and saying something about it. The second is that outlining in sentences allows you to begin developing relationships between your main ideas. Now, not everyone will be able to come up with the level of detail and sophistication that Jane manages at the outline level (at least not without some practice!), but her outline is living proof that A+ papers often begin at the outline level. And the third advantage is that the sentence outline is essentially a topic outline with *verbs*. But those verbs take you from simply having a topic to forcing you to say something about it.

Since outlines are formal processes, most outlines reveal the relationship between large topics, small subtopics, and individual examples using roman numerals, numbers, and letters in both upper and lower case forms. An explanation of the hierarchal structure follows and an example has been provided in Box 1.4.

The Outlining Process

1. Begin with a thesis statement. Your thesis statement should be as focused as possible and it should contain your essay's points of examination—at least three main points that you intend to prove or examine—as well as an assertion or argument.

2. Use a system that differentiates major points from supporting paragraphs that develop these points: Roman numerals (I, II, III, etc.) are major points that will be used to illustrate and prove the thesis statement. Upper-case letters (A, B, C, etc.) show the number of paragraphs that will be

used to illustrate each of the major points to be proven in the essay as set out by the thesis. Arabic numerals (1, 2, 3, etc.) are used to show the major examples for each topic sentence. Lower-case letters (a, b, c, etc.) are examples to the example, which we will explain further in number 4 below.

3. Break down each of your three main points into at least three major paragraphs. Each paragraph will have to have a specific and single focus and will have to be supported by at least three separate, specific, and significant examples. Usually, we like to say that one of the examples will elaborate on the topic sentence (a general statement that tells the reader what your paragraph is about), one will extend upon it, and the other will enhance it. Your paragraph should not simply be made up of a number of examples that repeat themselves—for example, a quote and then a reiteration of that quote in your own words. Although you may have these expressed as two separate sentences, you are ultimately still dealing with one *idea,* or one *example.*

4. Be as specific as possible in your outline and try to come up with an example:

> Anaphora is the repetition of a word or many words at the beginning of successive clauses. When used strategically, anaphora can create a wave-like effect building up the importance of a concept and creating a strong emotional affect; anaphora can also be used as a primary rhetorical device or style, setting a pace, creating a mood, building momentum, and raising importance: "The Lord sitteth above the water floods. The Lord remaineth a King forever. The Lord shall give strength unto his people. The Lord shall give his people the blessing of peace" (Psalm 29).

5. Remember that you are writing an outline, and not a rough draft of an essay. The outline should provide information in sentence form and not in complete paragraphs.

Title: The Role of Gender in Hong Kong Kung Fu Films

Thesis Statement: Martial arts films in Hong Kong have historically been enormously popular with both Chinese and Western audiences. However, unlike Hollywood action films, these films tend to have protagonists who achieve victory not only by being hyper-masculinised but also by embracing the traditional trait of masculine violence combined with the more feminine traits of mercy and compassion. Such a perspective recognizes that Chinese martial arts are based on the Taoist principle of yin and yang. Thus, the kung fu hero represents a philosophical fulfillment as a human being rather than an individual achieving revenge.

I. The history of Hong Kong action films.
   A. The historical differences between the Hollywood and Hong Kong systems.
      1. Subsidies and profits.
         a. Hong Kong represents non-subsidized, for-profit filmmaking.
         b. It is therefore dependent on low-budget, crowd-pleasing fare.
         c. Such entertainment has stemmed directly from the stylized genres of Chinese opera, which include action directly tied to an historical cultural knowledge.
   B. The independent players in the studios Golden Harvest and the Shaw Brothers.
      1. The 1970s birth of stars.
         a. Bruce Lee becomes a Chinese superstar by being both ethnically identified and a martial artist well known for his knowledge of philosophical grounding of the arts.
         b. The rise of Jackie Chan as Asia's most important star while running away from his fights, and his grounding in traditional opera.

C. Hong Kong cinema becomes an international force.
   1. In the beginning, many Asian markets in expatriate communities provide inroads internationally.
   2. Many disadvantaged communities, such as American inner-city black youth, found a strong appeal in the kung fu genre.

II. The roles played by males and females in these films.
   A. The de-sexualized monk.
      1. Typically in a role as a teacher.
      2. His purpose is to train the protagonist.
         a. The relationship is therefore paternal.
         b. The training can take on both physical and spiritual dimensions, often connecting the young protagonist to the teachings of Buddha and the core of martial arts.
   B. The feminized male traitor.
      1. Typically in the role as a turncoat, either to occupying forces such as the Japanese or to the other powers the protagonist struggles against.
      2. Purpose is as go-between among factions.
         a. The relationship is therefore "unnatural," often being depicted onscreen with homosocial overtones, with the protagonist typically ridding himself of this influence.
   C. The "kung fu mama."
      1. When present, females often fulfill the role of comrade-in-arms, fighting alongside other males, though rarely with the skill of the protagonist.
      2. Purpose is at most a chaste romance, and in some cases to enrage the protagonist to stop the antagonist due to overt brutality against the female character.
         a. There is a strong difference between the roles played by females in Hollywood action cinema and that of Hong Kong cinema, where they are often active participants in the combat.
         b. There are also cases of female antagonists, who tend to be more sexually charged than their protagonist counterparts.

D. The male protagonist.
   1. In classic kung fu cinema, the protagonist is usually young and chaste, sometimes to the extent of being a Buddhist monk.
      a. There is a long history of the Shaolin monk both in popular Chinese culture and in Hong Kong cinema.
   2. His purpose is typically to avenge some sort of extreme act by the antagonist against a particular group he identifies with: family, temple, village, or nation.
      a. In order to enact revenge, the antagonist should be destroyed.
      b. However, the protagonist must also be careful not to destroy himself in the process. By showing mercy, he will often allow the gods or the antagonist himself to guarantee a return to the natural order.
III. The basis of Chinese martial arts in the yin-yang principle.
   A. The Taoist principle of the rise of matter and the splitting into yin and yang.
      1. The origins of all things are based in the movement placed onto matter by the splitting of dark and light, cold and warmth, up and down, and male and female.
      2. As movement eventually becomes non-movement, stillness will become non-stillness.
         a. A film strictly following this Taoist philosophy would begin with harmony, develop disharmony, and move back to harmony.
         b. A character strictly following this philosophy would begin whole, become polarized, then have to regain wholeness.
         c. In most films, the audience has to imply the beginning harmony, and the progression is toward a return to that harmony.
   B. Tai chi and Wu shu (kung fu).
      1. Tai chi is the original martial art, with other forms of wu shu being elaborations on the philosophical postulate of yin and yang.
         a. Tai chi movement is to turn the attacker's energy back upon him or herself.

        b. Bagua stems from tai chi in that it is the further split of yin and yang into the eight trigrams, and the I Ching the combination of trigrams into hexagrams.

        c. All Chinese martial arts incorporate the hard and soft principles, with the softest being tai chi.

   C. The role of the teacher is paramount.

     1. The student and the teacher have responsibilities to each other.

        a. The student must practise diligently, both in outward forms of martial art and in philosophical development.

        b. The teacher must ensure that the student will use his or her knowledge wisely; in order to do this, the student must know right from wrong and must only use martial arts for good reason.

IV. The notion of the whole person as climactic achievement.

   A. The protagonist should not simply glory in vengeance but rather return to a state of stillness as per Taoist principles.

     1. There are many specific examples of the kung fu protagonist achieving victory through showing mercy to his opponent.

     2. Instead of getting the girl, the protagonist embodies the feminine traits he has utilized to achieve victory, thus becoming (half) the girl.

     3. In doing so, he returns to the original state as represented by the union of male and female to produce life, thus rejoining the Tao and giving the Chinese audience steeped in such philosophy a happy ending.

GRAMMAR **TIP**

Semicolons are great for separating two closely connected independent clauses, but don't use them too often. More than one per paragraph is distracting.

TYING IT ALL TOGETHER

For most students, pre-writing is a very difficult task—so difficult, in fact, that it is almost impossible to convince them to do it! However, pre-writing, as this chapter has set about showing, is an integral aspect of the writing and composing process. Pre-writing necessitates careful attention to detail. It allows that attention to detail without requiring perfection and meticulous invention. In fact, purpose statements and outlines force us as writers to make some very important strategic decisions up front: Why are we writing? And what are we writing about? Once we know the answer to those two questions, a careful outline is all we really need to help everything fall into place. Finally, since much of pre-writing is actually data collection, this stage also gives you an opportunity to see how others have approached the same topic, issue, or problem and to consider critically how you might approach the issue differently. What better way to learn than by example?

NOTES

1. Adapted from Rosenwasser, David, and Jill Stephen. *Writing Analytically with Readings*. Boston: Thomson Nelson, 2006. Print.

2. See Henderson, Eric. *Writing by Choice*. Don Mills, ON: Oxford University Press, 2006. Print, and Messenger, William, Jan de Bruyn, Judy Brown, and Ramona Montagnes. *The Canadian Writer's Handbook*. 5th ed. Don Mills, ON: Oxford University Press, 2008. Print.

3. *Purdue Online Writing Lab*. The Writing Lab and OWL at Purdue and Purdue U, 2011. Web. 2 Apr. 2011. <http://owl.english.purdue.edu/owl/resources>.

CHAPTER 2

Introductions and Thesis Statements

INTRODUCTIONS

How you begin and end your essay will impress your professor—or not—far more than everything in between. By the end of your introduction, your professor will have a fairly clear idea of what grade to give you, and your conclusion will be your last chance to improve that grade. But while learning to write great introductions and conclusions will make a dramatic difference in your essays, the first impression you make has more lasting effects, so your introduction is by far the most important paragraph of your essay.

Setting the Bar

There are several major differences between introductions in an A+ paper and those in B and C papers, and these differences typically reveal themselves in the first few sentences. One distinguishing characteristic of B and C papers is that they usually begin with a sentence or two of general contexts that are not fully developed in the paper's argument (*In today's society ...*), while A+ papers rarely take more than two or three sentences to set up the key problem or issue they will address. While the contexts of the B and C papers mainly introduce and, in the B papers, narrow a topic, excellent papers waste no time getting to their argument. To gain a clear idea not only of the differences between so-so introductions and great beginnings but also of how to get from one to the other, let's look at a few introductions, beginning with this C– introduction by Julie:

> Social status or class plays an important role throughout modern Canadian fiction. People in Canada struggle throughout the early twentieth century to distinguish not only what the national identity and structure might be, but also where they fit into that particular organization. Writers are no exception to this and we see in many modern novels the struggle of one or more characters to find their place within their society. In a new nation such as Canada, that doesn't necessarily have a developed social structure of its own, writers often feel a lack of belonging or a discontent with their own class, which shows in their work. There is also the issue of location, more than ever in a large area such as Canada; in many instances, especially in rural based narratives, survival outweighs the importance of the social structure and class becomes virtually non-existent—or perhaps it is simply overlooked in extenuating circumstances. Both the rural based <u>Wild Geese</u>, by Martha Ostenso, and the urban centred <u>Earth and High Heaven</u>, by Gwethalyn Graham, depict social structures through tensions between men and women, and religious differences. Graham and Ostenso took the issues of social status realistically when they developed their characters, and it is a key factor in how these characters think and act.

Before revising any piece of writing, it is a good practice to identify both what is not working and what is working because without some idea of what is worth keeping, you may delete too much and find yourself working backwards. So, first, what are the strengths of this introduction—the core ideas that we can build on? For one thing, the first sentence shows some promise because it introduces a claim that, if it can be elaborated on and given some credibility, could help explain some key issues in the novels the paper discusses. Also, the last two sentences propose the intended topic of the paper in some detail, and although there's no real argument just yet, there are glimpses of promise in the implication that rural and urban settings may affect how social tensions are represented in the novels.

Sticking Your Ideas Together: Being Cohesive and Coherent

The paragraph below resembles many undergraduate introductions in that its lack of purpose makes it impossible for it to be both *cohesive* and *coherent* at the same time. Coherence and cohesiveness are very useful concepts to employ as you write and edit because they are proven, reliable indicators of how clear your audience will find your writing. And although cohesiveness and coherence are distinguishing features of all clear communication, they are particularly vital characteristics of well-written introductions. Essentially, writing is cohesive when topical connections from sentence to sentence are clear, and it is coherent when your topics make sense as a whole. Generally, sentences make sense when they have clear topical and logical relations to the sentences that come before and after them (cohesiveness) and when all of the topics in a paragraph make sense as a whole (coherence). Consider, for example, this string of sentences:

> The vast majority of the Japanese populace lives in cities. Cities often have limited and overburdened social assistance resources for the disabled, the elderly, and the impoverished. Urban poverty is a mostly unacknowledged and insufficiently addressed problem in Japan, and if dramatic steps are not taken, the existing social assistance agencies in Japanese cities will soon be stretched beyond the point of bursting.

This example is cohesive because the main topic of each sentence has a clear connection to a topic in the sentence before it. It is not coherent, however, because we are not given a common thread that allows us to see all the topics as interconnected, as different, but interlocking, pieces of one puzzle. We get that the writer sees connections among urban population, urban poverty, and the strains upon social assistance agencies, but we have yet to be told how those topics relate to one another. If we had been given such an explanation, then this paragraph would be both *coherent* and *cohesive*.

Julie's paragraph in "Setting the Bar" suffers in cohesiveness because the main topics of each sentence relate ambiguously to their preceding sentences, and it suffers in coherence both because of that incohesiveness and because there are far more topics than this paragraph can possibly present in a clear and focused relationship. Both problems are common characteristics of first drafts, and the lack of clear topical connections between sentences results directly from a lack of purpose. It's natural for first drafts to have far more topics than the final draft, but when drafting your first introduction, you should be looking closely for any topics or ideas that don't have a direct relationship to your thesis statement. As you become a better editor of your own work, you will develop the ability to identify the topics that don't fit in your introduction, and to decide almost immediately whether they will work as supporting points later on or whether you will edit them out of your essay entirely.

Introductions that have clear thesis statements may sometimes suffer from some digression, but they are rarely this incohesive or incoherent, because *arguments make clear connections between topics*. In other words, the lack of a thesis is directly responsible for the surplus of topics and consequent lack of focus because having a strong purpose—knowing what you want to say—is the only way to make strong, clear connections between your ideas. That is why your thesis statement is so important. A great thesis brings all of your major topics together and animates your entire paper with a sense of purpose, but an ineffective thesis—and especially no thesis at all—will shroud your paper in a veil of purposelessness and ambiguity. Ambiguity will always result when you know what you want to talk about but haven't yet figured out your opinion on your topic. So the first step you must take before writing a great thesis statement is to commit to a position about your topic.

GENERATING FOCUS AND READER INTEREST

Great introductions begin by generating focus and reader interest, and having too many topics works against both. Julie's opening introduces far too many topics, thereby creating incoherence, as though she is telling the professor, "See? I've attended every lecture, and I know every topic on our syllabus!" Even worse, from the second sentence through to the last two, there is little or no sense of connection between the topics. This lack of sentence-to-sentence connection—what we called *incohesiveness*—thwarts the sense of connection and development that characterizes successful papers because unclear relations between topics means unclear connections between ideas. If your introduction is incohesive, your readers will not get a clear sense of how your ideas build on each other or relate together as a whole. So, to improve, we need to narrow the focus by removing the topics that aren't part of a main argument, then to create a clear sense of connection and sentence-to-sentence development by ensuring that the main topic of each sentence connects clearly to something before it.

This introduction has another problem that is typical of unsuccessful papers: although it's clear what the key words are, their meanings are ambiguous. The ambiguity begins in the first sentence, with "social status or class." Well, which is it? When introducing words and ideas that will figure prominently in your paper, it is crucial that you don't leave your audience with any questions about what those ideas mean, because if you leave any doubt about what an important word means, your audience can never be certain about what you are arguing. For instance, *social status* is a fairly general term, which in some disciplines could indicate a social position that is either earned or inherited. *Class*, on the other hand, distinctly suggests issues of struggle and social power, and possible relevance to Marxist theory, which this paper does not employ. Also, the ensuing mentions of "national identity and structure," "people in Canada," and "writers" do nothing to clarify those ambiguities, and if anything, they compound them.

It is important to note here that there is nothing wrong if your first draft contains many more ideas than you can tie together. In fact, generating an overabundance of topics through brainstorming is a great way to get your ideas on paper. But once that storm lets up, it's time to assess which topics should stay and which ones should not, and you decide that by evaluating which topics have the strongest connection to your argument. In this introduction, everything from "People in Canada" through to "extenuating circumstances" should be removed, except for the ideas about rural and urban narratives, which have some potential, however undeveloped, for being the subject of a thesis. All the extra topics create loose ends, and without a thesis statement tying everything together, the result for your reader will be confusion.

OPENING STRATEGIES

While there is no one strategy that will work for all introductions, there are a number of tested strategies for beginning essays. They each have particular advantages and disadvantages, and some hybrid approaches are possible (for instance, the startling statement may also be part of a funnel or inverted pyramid), but your purpose and your professor's requirements will determine

WRITING **TIP**

"Hook" your reader with something that would grab your interest as well. Think about the ways that a newspaper headline tries to make you read more—but beware of sounding too much like a tabloid!

to a large extent what type of opening is appropriate and effective. The following strategies are quite common.

The Overly General Statement

Don't begin with a context that is impossibly broad for your essay to discuss adequately. For example, "Throughout history, writers have been the voice of social conscience." This particular opening also exemplifies the "throughout history" (akin to the aforementioned "in today's society") opening, which you will be wise to avoid. For one thing, it introduces a time period (all of history) that is impossible to cover in even a 5000-word essay— let alone a 1500-word essay. And for another, your professors have seen this particular opening too many times before, and their gut reaction will be, "This is not looking good." Beginning your essay by introducing contexts and problems that your paper can't deal with in detail is typical of C papers, so don't use this opening if you're striving for an A paper.

The Startling Statement

Good introductions always have a strategy for catching their reader's attention. Most often, the interest is generated subtly through a relevant topic or a point of contention, but the startling statement aims to shock or provoke the reader into paying attention. For instance, "The intended target of the Americans' second nuclear bombing was not the primarily civilian hospital city of Nagasaki, but a military and industrial city named Kokuro." This type of opening typically has three distinct purposes: to catch the reader's attention, to introduce a context that relates directly to the paper's purpose, and to signal that the paper will somehow contest conventional wisdom. If you can craft a startling statement that performs those functions, and if you immediately develop how it sets up your main purpose, then use it.

An Analogy or Anecdote

Opening with an analogy can be a highly effective way to frame your purpose and to get to the crux of the problem you are discussing. But beware of drawn-out analogies or ones that introduce topics, contexts, or issues unrelated to your paper's purpose. Narrative openings or opening with an anecdote (a short story with a point) can be effective in assignments that allow for creative or personal expression, but you should always consult with your professor before using this strategy. But if you do, always use your opening to set out the main problems or issues, and follow up by illustrating how those ideas bear directly on your core argument.

The Procedural Opening

In this strategy, which you would usually use after a thesis statement rather than at the beginning of your introduction, you tell your professor exactly where your paper will go and why. For instance, "This paper will be broken down into three main sections. Part one will…. Part two will … and part three will…. This paper will close with a discussion of the findings and considerations for future research." Although many find this approach dry and mechanical, it does spell out for your reader exactly what you intend to do and how you intend to do it, and in some social sciences classes, you may be required to use specific versions of the procedural opening. Also, this opening works well in conjunction with other openings: if you began with an anecdote or a startling statement and you're not sure if your professor sees where you're going with your idea, the procedural opening is a great way to spell it out so that even the densest professor can't help but catch your drift.

Beginning with a Definition

Beware: this opening can go over very well or very badly, and some professors love this opening while others despise it. If you feel compelled to use this opening, be very aware of its advantages and pitfalls. At its worst, it can simply be a cliché, one that is every bit as tired as "It is said that a picture can speak a thousand words" (which is another opening to avoid like the plague). The most hated version of this opening is, for many professors, the dreaded Webster's, Wikipedia, or Dictionary.com definition, which may clear up the meaning of a word but does little if anything to grab your reader's attention, at least not in any constructive way. Also, it gives you little to work with. Consider the Dictionary.com definition of *metaphor*: "a figure of speech in which a term or phrase is applied to something to which it is not literally applicable in order to suggest a resemblance, as in 'A mighty fortress is our God.'"* Even if you are writing a paper about metaphor, you gain little from quoting this, as this is a barebones, common-knowledge version of the word. Your professor doesn't need to be told it, and you've just wasted your one shot at an impressive entrance. Sometimes, however, a more sophisticated, specialist dictionary or encyclopedia entry may do the trick, especially if it introduces a key issue or problem that your paper will pounce on and respond to. Compare the Dictionary.com definition to this opening, which is taken from an A paper by Robert:

> The New Princeton Encyclopedia of Poetry and Poetics defines metaphor as:
> ... a trope, or figurative expression, in which a word or phrase is shifted from its normal use to a context where it evokes new meanings. When the ordinary meaning of a word is at odds with the context, we tend to seek relevant features of the word and the situation that will reveal the intended meaning.† (Preminger et al. 760)

Beginning with such a long quote is a risky move, but in a paper that extended this definition into a theory that poetic metaphors do not have one fixed meaning but a field of meanings, the move paid off. The introduction was critical to the development of the paper, as the ensuing sentences drew out the main areas of interest (the departure from a static context and the

RESEARCH **TIP**

General encyclopedias (including Wikipedia) are a good starting point for background information on a topic, but they rarely make good citations. Most professors do not appreciate references to them (nor copying from them!).

---

*Definition of metaphor, Dictionary.com, 2011.
†*The New Princeton Encyclopedia of Poetry and Poetics* (1993). Alex Preminger & T.V.F. Brogan, Frank J. Warnke, O. B. Hardison, Jr., and Earl Miner, Associate Editors. Princeton University Press.

role of an active reader), then quickly and efficiently laid out the gaps in the definition before ending with a working hypothesis of how metaphors work in the poetry of Wilfred Owen.

The Logical Approach

Often called the deductive approach, the "funnel," or the inverted pyramid (picture a tornado or a yield sign), this tactic begins with a general or universal—but not broad and overstated—statement and leads up to the thesis statement. Papers that use this approach provide a conceptual context for the entire essay to follow; they often begin with a theory or idea, then apply it to a specific phenomenon. When used effectively, the logical approach gives the reader a conceptual tool for navigating complex issues. An aptly introduced theory or concept can centre your discussion, mapping out connections between topics, even if your essay will focus on qualifying and even contradicting some points of the central theory.

Opening with a Quotation

If you observe several guidelines, this can be a fairly safe, yet highly effective, opening. The most important guideline is never to quote more than you can engage with immediately; that guideline holds true for all the paragraphs in your essay, but there is far less opportunity for digression in your introduction. The goal when beginning with a quotation is to introduce your framing idea while providing the quickest path possible to your thesis. So, if you feel tempted to begin by quoting an entire paragraph from Rousseau's "Discourse on Inequality," don't. You'd be far better off choosing the one sentence that best introduces your main contexts or frames your argument or beginning with a summary of a key concept, mostly or all in your words. Of course, if you do that, you must distinguish his ideas from yours—and "According to Rousseau ..." is an excellent way to accomplish that.

THESIS STATEMENTS

Most students expend a considerable amount of energy finding and researching a topic. In fact, many students never get past

BOX 2.1 SUMMARY OF OPENING STRATEGIES

So while there are many ways to go about writing an introduction, there are several firm principles, and if you observe them, you will have written a really good introduction.

- Use your opening sentence to get your audience's attention, to introduce only contexts and topics that are crucial to your argument, and to get to, or at least approach, the *central problem or issue* that your paper will be dealing with.

- Ensure that you maintain *cohesiveness* and *coherence* by introducing only topics that have built-in connections to your thesis statement and by making sure that the main topic of each sentence has a clear connection to something in the previous sentence.

- Communicate *your purpose* clearly. Essays succeed when they communicate great ideas and have a clear thesis. But for your professor to recognize your brilliance, you must introduce your thesis carefully and without digression. Your introduction will work when it consists only of a great thesis and everything your professor needs to comprehend it.

- Whether you connect your ideas to a scholarly issue or you use an analogy, theory, or quote, there must be something *to frame* your idea and make it relevant.

their topic until, often at 2 a.m. on the day of the deadline, they end up writing introductions without thesis statements and essays without discernible arguments. Your professors or TAs will not be reading your introduction simply to know your topic but to determine and assess your thesis: *a clear statement of your arguable opinion on the topic.* But how *do* you get from a topic to a thesis? Though there are several means of getting there, the most effective means is through an *issue* (or *problem*).

Opening with an issue or problem that your audience knows or can quickly be taught facilitates the transition into your thesis statement for two reasons. First, it minimizes the amount of contextual information that you must communicate, and, second, it involves dynamic and easily grasped relations between *ideas* and *positions*. Also, in academic contexts, if you can find an issue within a topic, you will also find a number of different responses to the issue. Therefore, finding your argument can be as simple as siding—more or less—with one of those responses and justifying your position using different reasons.

Grounded in a clear problem, your thesis statements will strike your readers with maximum impact because the dimensions of your problem will encourage and enable your readers to actively engage with the issue and think along with you. But best of all, problems or issues are very often ready-made for further debate: a good thesis rarely results from a prodigious leap of intuition but most often is simply a concise statement of the writer's response to a problem. And generally, the more clearly and boldly you can state your opinion or position on a well-defined problem, the better your thesis will be. In fact, of all the papers that are written over a pot of coffee on the night of a deadline, the worst are written "about a topic." The ones that take a strong, reasonably informed position on a scholarly, course-related issue, then defend it tooth and nail for the balance of the word limit generally do fairly well.

Why Thesis Statements Are So Important

Without a doubt, the thesis statement is the most important sentence in every essay. An effective thesis statement states the entire argument of the paper in a nutshell, and it navigates both writers and readers through the paper while tying all of the major ideas of the paper together. Think of your thesis statement as a snapshot of your whole paper or as the instructions for assembling a complex item of furniture: it explains how all the parts fit together. When you open the packaging for an item of flat-packed furniture, the first thing you do is look for the assembly instructions or diagram. In very much the same way, when your professor begins reading your paper, the first thing she will look for is the thesis statement that will tell her not only what argument you will be building, but how you intend to prove it. Thus, reading a paper with no thesis feels like opening a box containing a jumble of nuts, bolts, and boards but lacking instructions about how the pieces are supposed to go together or even what you are supposed to be assembling.

So it is no coincidence that papers lacking a thesis statement also tend to lack any discernible argument and that thesis-less papers are typically disorganized and unfocused throughout. In short, they are terrible papers. While having a thesis statement does not guarantee that the paper will succeed (basing an essay on flawed assumptions or plagiarizing someone else's work are just two of many ways to go horribly wrong), merely including a thesis statement in your introduction does dramatically increase the potential of your paper by giving your audience—and yourself—a clear idea of what the purpose of the paper is. Professors and writing instructors routinely answer more questions about thesis statements than about any other sentence in an essay. Here are some examples of the typical questions students ask and the probable responses they may encounter:

Q: Why do I need to have a thesis statement anyway? Can't you tell where I'm going with my topic?

A: Without a clear statement of your paper's precise aims, it is difficult to determine what they are. In fact, if you cannot tell us your purpose, then we cannot be certain that you really have one.

Q: Is it okay just to tell you my topic, then to get around to my views on it later?

A: In your first draft, that is a sound approach. The purpose of your first draft is to discover your argument by exploring your topic and by testing hypotheses through analysis to determine what does and does not work. So, your first draft is written entirely for you to discover and develop your argument. But your final draft is written for your audience, and your audience is looking for a thesis statement.

Q: What makes a thesis statement different from the other sentences in my introduction—how do you know when you're reading a thesis statement?

A: Two things. One, while the other sentences introduce necessary contexts for the thesis, the thesis statement actually makes a claim that the rest of the paper will need to validate. Two, because the purpose of the introduction culminates in the thesis, we expect the thesis to be near, and usually at, the end of your introduction.

Q: How much of my grade rides on the thesis?

A: Ultimately, a lot. The thesis statement is usually a barometer of an essay's success because it tells us what the rest of the paper will do, or at least will try to do.

GETTING FROM YOUR TOPIC TO YOUR THESIS

Successful essays go beyond demonstrating knowledge of a topic, and they do that by taking a stance on an issue. Coming up with a good thesis statement is all about getting from your topic (what you are talking about) to your thesis (your stance, what you have to say about it). Consider the following topics:

- second-hand smoking

- racism in Joseph Conrad's *Heart of Darkness*[1]

- mandating 100 percent renewable household energy

All three are interesting and suggestive topics, and the more familiar you become with research on these topics, the more you will become aware of different and conflicting opinions on them.

Such topics are ideal for writing about, as they are open to a range of possible responses and the issues are far from settled. It is far more difficult to enter debates on such topics as religion, abortion, or the death penalty because, although they are also still being debated, you are unlikely to be able to change anyone's beliefs on the topic. Likewise, it is difficult to discuss how good Shakespeare's plays are or how socially beneficial the feminist movement has been because social and critical opinions are quite agreed on those matters and because arguments of value tend to be very subjective and therefore difficult to prove.

So, how do we take these three topics and turn them into thesis statements? The first step is to find an issue that divides opinions. With the first topic, writers must be wary of polarizing their audience, and keen students may realize that this issue is really about balancing the rights of smokers to smoke and the rights of non-smokers to not be smoked upon. With the second topic, a quick read of the novel and even just a cursory research of the scholarly literature on it will reveal, among many other issues, that there is a question of whether the racist representation in the novel negates the literary value of Conrad's text. And with the third topic, you could choose to balance the pressing need to protect the environment against the economic realities of homeowners and all taxpayers, few of whom are financially equipped (or willing) to burden the costs of implementing clean energy.

For some short, first-year essays of around 750 words, it may be enough at this point to take a side, then give your reasons. Even in those essays, however, good grades will depend upon your ability to establish that your argument is not motivated by subjective concerns (for instance, that you're a smoker, you hate racism, or you're a card-carrying member of Greenpeace). Surprising as it may seem, your professors are not looking for a "right" answer that confirms what they believe but rather for an argument that is based on facts, consistent with relevant research, and argued reasonably and creatively, with due respect paid to all sides of the issue. At this point, therefore, while many students may already have a fairly good idea of where they stand on the issue, savvy students will look for a framing idea—a theory or statement that connects the elements of their problem while providing a principle that will facilitate their analysis.

Framing as Strategy

Using a framing idea accomplishes two things. It helps you to communicate the connections between your ideas clearly, and especially if the idea you use is a theory with some scientific or scholarly merit, it signals that your analysis is based upon objective, scientific principles. Also, the theory you use—and a *theory* is simply something that explains how something works—can provide your means of analyzing data in your body paragraphs. One key aspect of framing ideas is that they can be something that your professor, or another professor writing about the same issue, has not thought about: as long as you can defend the relevance and applicability of that framework, then you will have given your audience another way of thinking about the issue, and that is likely to raise the value of your analysis.

Here are possible working theses for the three topics we have been looking at. Note that all three use some sort of framing idea that indicates to the audience how the paper will set about proving its claim.

The federal government should limit smoking in public places because smoking has been proven to cause illness and death in smokers and non-smokers alike.

While Joseph Conrad's *Heart of Darkness* has a long history of literary acclaim, the many racist characteristics of its narrative at the very least demand recognition in how it is taught and raise serious questions about the high critical status it has been accorded in the canon of English literature.

While the economic costs of immediately mandating 100 percent renewable household energy are untenable for the vast majority of taxpayers, the current methods of producing household energy are environmentally unsustainable; the federal government must therefore implement a comprehensive plan to achieve 100 percent renewable energy by 2020 to protect our environment while not overburdening taxpayers.

As the first example demonstrates, the framing of ideas can be implicit, as long as the ideas are clear. In that instance, the mention of the government signals that any issues of right or wrong will be analyzed from an objective, legal perspective, and the qualifier "in public places" indicates that the right of smokers to smoke in the privacy of their own homes will be respected. In the second example, the author approaches the thorny issue of art and morality by framing the issue as "at least" worthy of more consideration at the level of education; doing so opens up some space for discussing the status of Conrad's novel as "great" literature but without alienating the many critics who see great literary value in the novel. The third thesis is a little long, but it is not uncommon for a thesis statement to be the longest sentence of an essay because it needs to pack in an argument, a perspective on an issue, and some indication of the author's reasoning. In the third example, the framing idea is sheer pragmatism; both sides may have a point, but immediate action is necessary, and for that to happen, compromise is necessary.

FIXING THESIS STATEMENTS

The thesis statement is the most important sentence in an essay precisely because it encapsulates the entire argument and purpose of the paper into one sentence. The problem is, however, that it usually takes several drafts to figure out exactly what you will be arguing. So it makes sense that your thesis statement should change significantly from draft to draft. As you gain a better and better sense of what you want to accomplish with your paper, your thesis should grow to reflect your improved sense of purpose.

Unfortunately, many students are afraid of tinkering with thesis statements, and as a result, their professors end up reading papers that begin with a muddled or vague sense of purpose, then acquire some clarity around midway, and in the end leave them with numerous questions about the student's whole argument—

for instance, whether the paper actually established the claim it declared or whether it went off on a coherent tangent. The result is, at best, a B, but with a little understanding of how to fix thesis statements and recalibrate introductions accordingly, the result could have been much better.

We have said that good thesis statements are essentially an entire argument in a nutshell; it makes sense, then, that your thesis should contain some of your major ideas and should convey something about how everything fits together logically. A+ thesis statements differ from C+ statements in their very grammar (i.e., their sentence DNA—see Chapter 8), and every difference enables the sentence to communicate more about the greater purpose of the paper and to do it clearly. Here are several of those critical differences.

Effective thesis statements use *dependent clauses*, which communicate crucial information about the sentence. A simple grammatical fact makes this a very critical difference: dependent clauses begin with *subordinating conjunctions*, which express logical connections between the main sentence and the dependent clause. For instance, a clause beginning with *because* answers the question "Why?" while a clause beginning with *by* will answer the question of "How?" Dependent clauses can be placed at the end of sentences, or even at the beginning, where an "although" clause can establish a productive contrast between the thesis statement and the sentence immediately preceding it. See Chapter 8 for more on clause types.

Effective thesis statements incorporate complexity without sacrificing clarity. After all, if your big idea is a lot more than a simplistic statement of fact, then your thesis statement should

---

GRAMMAR **TIP**

Logical relationships within a sentence are realized by conjunctions. Coordination (putting items on the same grammatical level) is most commonly achieved with *and*, *but*, and *or*. Subordination has vastly more terms, but is commonly achieved with *although*, *because*, *if*, *since*, and *when*—depending on the kind of logic you wish to engage in.

---

reflect that. Dependent clauses are excellent at improving both clarity and complexity, but there is another technique: the two-part thesis, which uses two linked *independent clauses* (i.e., clauses that could be sentences by themselves) to communicate a fuller sense of the paper's purpose. Here, in an essay by Sarah on Chaucer's "House of Fame,"[2] is an excellent example of the two-part thesis at work.

> The narrator's relationship with his own story not only gives the entire poem its unique and entertaining style, but also comprises the most significant structure device in the poem; indeed, Chaucer's narrator is a living example that life not only imitates art but is made by it.

In this example, the semicolon is used with excellent results to punctuate that the ideas of this sentence (too many for one simple sentence) have been divided neatly into two contrasting statements: the first asserts the importance of the narrator's role while the second extends the comparison into an argument about art, imitation, and life. The two-part thesis has other uses as well. You can use a colon followed by a brief list of major points (i.e., the procedural thesis), or you can begin with a general or theoretical idea and then apply it specifically and argumentatively to your topic.

In clear and powerful thesis sentences, the most important ideas are always in the main clause, and they usually coincide with the headwords of the subject, verb, and (where applicable) object. For instance, consider this thesis statement from an analytical paper. It contains a good idea, but it puts all the most important words in all the wrong places.

> Mikhail Bakhtin, in his book called *The Dialogic Imagination*, asserts that, when we try to communicate to other people, our perceptions and preconceptions about them form a barrier that must first be transcended.

The main idea of the Bakhtin[3] reading is the bit about interpersonal communication, but it is lost inside the object (the large clause beginning with *that*) in a "when clause," which we know is a dependent clause. However, it is a key idea of what Bakhtin argues, so it should be in the main clause of the object. Observe

Introductions and Thesis Statements **49**

the difference in clarity and impact when we simply put the right words in the right places:

> Bakhtin argues in *The Dialogic Imagination* that we communicate by crossing the boundaries of our perceptions and preconceptions.

In fact, that simple adjustment worked so well that the sentence now seems too simple; in other words, we have opened up some space in the sentence structure for some dependent clauses that can make the sentence say *even* more.

THE THESIS IS THE DOORWAY TO YOUR ESSAY

When first-year students hear the word *thesis*, their first response is often confusion or, when asked to give an example, pure panic. But once they think about that sentence that they need to have in their introduction as a *hypothesis*, the word becomes far less mystical and intimidating. Thinking of the statement as a hypothesis enables exploration of an issue, while imparting a scientific and logical sensibility to that exploration. A hypothesis is also more than a topic or even an opinion, as it suggests a logical, scientific inquiry that is geared toward a conclusion. A hypothesis is also flexible, as it can and should sustain some testing, and possibly refining or revision, along the way. It imparts both impetus and direction to the essay because it makes a claim that the rest of your essay must prove while giving your audience some sense of both the manner and appropriateness of your approach.

Your thesis is the doorway to the rest of your essay, a concept that we will cover in more depth in Chapter 5 on discussions, and Chapter 6 on conclusions. Your thesis can also become a powerful tool for organizing your essay, but only if you use it to crystallize your purpose in the essay. As the sample of typical questions and answers about thesis statements showed, your professors value your thesis statements very highly, and so should you. Use your thesis to make a claim that makes your opinion somehow unique, sets out clearly what the rest of your essay will prove, and gives your audience a sense that you understand the issue and have something worthwhile to say about it. If you can write thesis statements that do those things well, you will be on your way toward writing a really good essay.

NOTES

1. Conrad, Joseph. *Heart of Darkness*. Norton Critical Edition. Ed. Paul B. Armstrong. New York: W.W. Norton, 2005. Print.

2. Chaucer, Geoffrey, "The House of Fame." *The Complete Works of Geoffrey Chaucer*. Ed. W.W. Skeat. Oxford: Clarendon Press, 1899. Print. A copy of the text is available online at The Online Medieval and Classical Library <http://omacl.org/Houseoffame/>. Web.

3. Bakhtin, M.M. *The Dialogic Imagination: Four Essays*. Ed. Michael Holquist, Ed. and Trans. Vadim Liapunov, and Trans. Kenneth Brostrum. Austin, TX: University of Texas Press Slavic Series, 1981. Print.

Writing Body Paragraphs

BEGINNING AT THE BEGINNING: SO, WHAT IS A PARAGRAPH?

A paragraph is probably best described as a group of sentences that is organized coherently and controlled by some general organizing structure. A paragraph is a paragraph because it is complete, because it makes sense, and because it is tied together using words that help the ideas in the structure—the paragraph—flow and move forward. The realization of *completeness* is intimately connected to cohesion, structure, and information.

WRITING **TIP**

A good paragraph is a structured paragraph. It is cohesive and it makes a point, much like an essay. It has a topic sentence, it has a body that is well developed, and it offers some type of conclusion that integrates the paragraph into main purpose of the essay. Most importantly, good paragraphs develop the argumentative thesis statement: the point that is going to be argued and proven in the remainder of the essay.

Paragraph Roles

Paragraphs contribute various types of information to an essay. What information they contain has everything to do with your audience and the main claim of your essay (yes, your thesis). Regardless of whether a paragraph is meant to be comparative, process-oriented, or purely definitional, all paragraphs in a solid academic paper share one common characteristic: they all have a controlling idea, typically delivered via a topic sentence.

IT'S ALL ABOUT THE TOPIC SENTENCE

In the simplest of terms, many writers understand topic sentences to be general opening sentences that define the topic and purpose of each paragraph. The topic sentence also has a number of important tasks: it must provide an organizing structure to the paragraph and it should refer back to the thesis statement, in some way contributing to it by making relevant how the paragraph will develop the argument set out in the thesis. The topic sentence needs to be broad enough to be developed sufficiently; it cannot be a simple statement of fact, and it must therefore be *arguable*. To be arguable, your topic sentence just needs to leave room for explanation or for other points of view, which of course is what the rest of your paragraph needs to do.

Problems occur when (a) a writer fails to include a topic sentence—a general opening statement telling the reader what the paragraph is about or (b) the paragraph does not actually fulfill what the topic sentence promises. The first of these two problems is self-explanatory, but the second merits further elaboration. When a paragraph is not on the same topic as the topic sentence, we say that it has not fulfilled its promise. Often this happens because the topic sentence turns out to be too general or too specific and leaves either more to explain than anyone can possibly explain in one paragraph or not enough to say about the topic. As instructors, we can usually trace long, rambling paragraphs back to an overly general topic sentence, and overly short paragraphs to topic sentences that make a simple statement of fact. In other words, your topic sentences have a significant impact on the shape and effectiveness of the entire paragraph.

A CAUTIONARY EXAMPLE OF TRYING TO
GRAB TOO MUCH

Monkeys show us at an essential level what it means to be human. We are well aware that they are social animals, and thus the way that they organize their socialization is important. It is well known that bonobos are not only the most linguistically advanced species of non-human primate, but also the most highly sociosexual in behaviour (de Waal 82[1]). However, recent research has also revealed that they kill and eat other monkeys (Kaplan par. 2[2])! This behaviour brings up interesting questions on how sex, language, and violence are linked.

Note: *This topic—what it means to be human—is simply too much for an essay, and its connection to socio-sexuality, language, and intra-primate murder is a bit of a leap unless you have a whole book to write!*

Writing Effective Topic Sentences and Supporting Them with Appropriate Examples

Some of you may be surprised that there is so much research on topic sentences, but there is, and we will now share some of the highlights. Margaret van Dijk (232)[3] makes the important point that effective topic sentences do two things at once: they state the point about the paragraph (what the paragraph will set out to prove, discuss, illustrate, etc.) while maintaining the reader's focus on the wider issue, which is the thesis statement, the reason why you are attempting to create such poignant paragraphs to develop and ultimately make your point. Similarly, Kane and Pyrcz (227)[4] observe that a topic sentence is good when it is only as long as an idea requires. Their example: "Trees work for a living" (Midge Ellis Keeble qtd. in Kane and Pyrcz 226). The topic sentence above is a formidable example: it is strong, clear, and general enough to allow the writer to support and illustrate the assertion with appropriate examples that will ultimately create an effective paragraph. In other words, it begins and structures an argument that defines the paragraph. To put it another way, this topic sentence expresses the purpose of its

> ## GRAMMAR **TIP**
>
> Your verb should agree with the head of the nominal group comprising your subject, not with the qualifier. "A barrel of monkeys are exciting" is thus incorrect; the sentence should read, "A barrel of monkeys is exciting." *Barrel* is your subject head, not *monkeys*.

paragraph, much like a thesis statement expresses the purpose of an essay.

Topic sentences should *not* be

- statements of facts (examples) because examples usually don't need further qualification of any in-depth sort.

- located at the end of paragraphs—particularly in academic grade papers (true, the paragraphs in creative works might build paragraphs up to a topic sentence, but we maintain that excellent academic essays are excellent because they are clear right off the bat!)

- fragments, that is, partial ideas, sometimes punctuated for dramatic effect. Writers in some genres prefer topic sentences of this sort. But you must remember to always keep your audience in mind: academic papers have professors as their primary audience, and we don't like sentence fragments!

The consensus in the literature is that poor topic sentences cannot be developed sufficiently in an academic paper. The best types of topic sentences are general enough to allow for at least three well-developed examples in a paragraph that is about one-half of a page (ideally about six sentences) in length.

USING EXAMPLES EFFECTIVELY

Academic essays are academic because of how they are written. How a writer presents information in a paragraph speaks volumes about that writer's ethos, or credibility. Paragraphs that are organized and structured with a specific focus in mind and that use information that elaborates, expands, and enhances upon the topic sentence are more refined than paragraphs that do not. In fact, as you will see later in this chapter, we can take the most simple topic and write a very eloquent paragraph if we adhere to, or at the very least respect, some simple rules: namely, that a paragraph must be developed using at least three very specific, significant, and single examples. Each of these examples, whenever possible, should also have some backing of its own in the form of further quotes, facts, or examples. We recommend, therefore, choosing examples that explicitly explain, exemplify, or expand on the topic.

Elaboration, Extension, and Enhancement

Listen carefully to these words of Halliday and Matthiessen: "Paragraphs should be developed with a focus on how one might enrich a building, either by (i) elaborating its existing structure; (ii) extending it by addition or replacement; (iii) enhancing its

---

WRITING TIP

So, how long should a paragraph be?

- Paragraphs need to be long enough to make a point, illustrate and prove it, and then show how the paragraph supports and develops the main idea expressed in the thesis. You can't do all that properly in two sentences. So, if you have a topic sentence and a conclusion, with one sentence each for three points that illustrate, support, and develop the topic sentence, then five sentences is the minimum length of an effective paragraph.

- Writing guides vary, but most recommendations for paragraph length vary from 5 to 10 sentences for regular paragraphs, with 8 to 12 being recommended for extended paragraphs. If you aim to have most of your paragraphs between 6 and 8 sentences, you will strike a good balance between developing your ideas and maintaining coherence.

Writing Body Paragraphs **57**

environment" (395).[5] For those who prefer a more concrete definition, you may consider examples that *elaborate* to be those which somehow restate or specify the topic sentence in greater detail, often through illustration or definition. In contrast, examples of *extension* often add to the topic sentence by providing some new element for consideration. Sometimes, this new element provides comparison or contrast. Examples of extension are powerful, and they often allow the writer to present another point of view—which is a useful and necessary manoeuvre in persuasive paragraphs. Finally, examples that *enhance* the topic sentence often provide information that somehow qualifies the topic sentence by providing a significant context, such as cause, condition, or place. Often, the conjunctive adjuncts *so, yet,* or *then* are used to introduce this type of information.

We will examine below how we can further apply the principles of elaboration, extension, and enhancement to paragraph development, under the discussion of paragraph development and logic.

COHESION AND COHERENCE IN PARAGRAPH STRUCTURE

Cohesion and coherence has to do with how a paragraph (and ultimately an essay) *hangs together*. This act requires that the words in the paragraph not only make sense (and are thus coherent), but also flow and are connected logically. *Cohesion* is the word we use when talking about this sentence-to-sentence flow—the sense of unbroken connection between sentences and their ideas.

Cohesion through Repetition

Cohesion can be realized using many strategies, but we will start you off with six.

1. *reiteration* (exact repetition of words)

2. *repetition* using similar words and ideas, also known as *synonymy* (words with essentially the same meaning: *come, arrive*)

3. *antonymy* (words with opposite meaning: *come, go*)

4. *hyponymy* (words related by category–member relationship: *travel, leave*)

5. *metonymy* (words with whole–part relationship: *hand, finger; finger, thumb*)[6]

6. *integration* of transition terms or phrases in order to help move the paragraph along

Remember, however, that a good paragraph is very different from a good recipe. While both have similar characteristics in that they provide the necessary information to complete a task or to come to a final understanding, good paragraphs do much more than simply present their information; they do it in a fluid fashion.

Cohesion through Connection

We mentioned above that transitions are those words or phrases that connect ideas in the form of sentences, to keep them flowing. Grammatically, transitions are usually in the form of conjunctive adverbs or phrases. These conjunctive adverbs, or transition words, supply the writer with a multitude of ways to express connections between sentences and their ideas. We can express these connections in a number of various ways, as this chart adapted from Halliday and Matthiessen (82) illustrates.

TABLE 3.1

Type	Meaning	Examples
appositive	that is (i.e.) or for example (e.g.)	that is, in other words; for instance
corrective	rather	or rather, at least, to be precise
dismissive	in any case	in any case, anyway, leaving that aside
summative	in short	briefly, to sum up, in conclusion
verificative	actually	actually, in fact, as a matter of fact
additive	and	also, moreover, in addition, besides
adversative	but	on the other hand, however, conversely

(continued)

TABLE 3.1 (*continued*)

Type	Meaning	Examples
variative	instead	instead, alternatively
temporal	then	meanwhile, before that, later on, next, soon, finally
comparative	likewise	likewise, in the same way
causal	so	therefore, for this reason, as a result, with this in mind
conditional	(if …) then	in that case, under the circumstances, otherwise
concessive	yet	nevertheless, despite that
respective	as to that	in this respect, as far as that's concerned

Source: M.A.K Halliday and C.M.I.M Matthiessen. *An Introduction to Functional Grammar,* 3rd ed. Pg. 82. London: Arnold. Reproduced by permission of Hodder Education.

Conjunctive adverbs can be placed between sentences, at the beginning of sentences, or even at the beginning of clauses within sentences—especially after semicolons, to improve the flow of a paragraph.

Textual Cohesion: What Comes First and What Follows

What makes a paragraph flow, connect, and make sense? It has everything to do with what comes first and what comes immediately before and after every sentence in the paragraph. We said at the beginning of this chapter that the topic sentence is the most important sentence in a paragraph because it provides an organizing structure to the text and tells the reader what to expect. Good paragraphs fulfill the expectations of the topic sentence by creating other sentences organized in a logical manner that follows a specific pattern: what functional grammarians have coined the Given–New relationship and what rhetoricians and writing instructors call the Known–New Contract. Essentially, they are talking about the same idea: given (known) information comes first because it provides the context needed for developing the clause's message and because it leads the reader to some new and dynamic idea not yet known to the reader.

DEVELOPING PARAGRAPHS LOGICALLY THROUGH DEFINITION, EXPLANATION, AND QUALIFICATION

Most academic paragraphs benefit from, and are in fact predicated on, sound logical development. Logical development actually refers only to the manner in which a paragraph is developed; hence, academic paragraphs develop the topic sentence by focusing on consequences or definitions and by dividing the topic sentence into various parts and then subsequently analyzing those parts to develop the position made in the topic sentence. We shall look at each method separately.

Development Using Definitions

Paragraph development using definition as the main strategy aims to explain the meaning of a word, concept, or idea. How you prepare your paragraph using definition as your organizational tool has everything to do with what your audience expects and knows. Once you are familiar with the reader's expectations and you have a concrete thesis statement, developing the paragraph using definition as your tool takes a very straightforward approach. First, use the topic sentence to introduce the term and set up the context by which to offer the definition. Then, based on your audience analysis and your audience expectations, decide whether it is best to offer a definition by *synonym*, a definition by *negation,* or a definition by *category*.

A definition by synonym illustrates and subsequently enhances the original meaning of the term. Often, synonyms are helpful when the original concept is difficult and a synonym offers a more comprehensible explanation. "She is claustrophobic, which means afraid of enclosed spaces."

A definition by negation explains the idea of the term by focusing on what something does not mean. By highlighting what something is not, the writer draws the importance of the term to the reader's attention. "Marriage is not the end of single life; it is the beginning of partnership."

A definition by category explains an idea, term, or concept by categorizing it into some larger whole so that it is easily accessible. Definitions by category are very important in academic writing because professors pay very close attention to whether you classify your information into taxonomies that are both internally consistent and consistent with relevant research. Classification and categorization usually occurs by focusing on characteristics that are easily recognizable to the average reader. "A nurse is an individual who has been trained to care for the sick." Naturally, we might develop this paragraph further with appropriate examples illustrating the types of nurses there are: registered nurse, licensed practical nurse, or registered psychiatric nurse, as well as by department or specialty, such as emergency room, pediatric intensive care, or neonatal.

In all cases, examples make up the heart of the paragraph. Examples must be significant, single, and specific, and they should not be a repetition of the same idea in different words. Examples should always develop the general topic sentence by providing elaboration, enhancement, and extension.

Development Using Explanation

Developing a paragraph using an explanation is a useful way to begin, especially when the topic of your paragraph is somehow abstract in nature. For example, let us say that the paragraph is about the topic of love. Love can mean many different things to many different readers, and in various contexts it can be explained differently and with important variances in meaning and affect. When we want to explain the importance of an abstract concept, it is often important to call upon our creative drive: metaphor and simile can be a useful means of expressing something in a clear fashion. An example of this is Robert Burns's famous "My love is like a red, red rose." Sometimes, explanations take the form of *illustrations*: examples that draw on the senses to show

how love can be depicted. For instance, you could illustrate the concept of love figuratively or expressively in a way that would be impossible using definition alone.

Development Using Qualification

Qualifying something means drawing the reader's attention to an idea or point that can be developed through the appearance of contraction. Often, writers begin by pointing out something that is generally true, but that can be developed further using varying examples to make a strong point. For instance, "*Although* women have, *overall*, moved up in the world in terms of earning *more* competitive salaries, in some professions, *very* little has changed." Qualification allows the writer to develop a point by presenting the most important issue, often at the end. This draws the reader's focus to the main dynamic point: that little has changed in the realm of women and work. This paragraph could then be neatly developed by providing three specific examples and elaborating on each by providing the supports necessary to make it convincing.

ORGANIZING THE PARAGRAPHS

Although examples and illustrations that provide the necessary data to support the topic sentence are the most important paragraph building units, organization is also important and should not be left to chance. Essentially, most writers will admit that organization is what helps a reader move through a paragraph with ease. If a reader must stop, reread, and think about an idea or proposition that has been presented, the reading process has been marred. Excellent essays are based on excellent organization of the information presented in each of the body paragraphs. Preparing to write an excellent paragraph, like many activities, takes time and practice. It usually involves more than one draft, but some helpful tips can make the process easier to master.

Plan Your Writing Process to Consist of Several Distinct Steps

First, simply write down what you are thinking without worrying about organization and presentation. Begin writing with the recognition that editing and restructuring will have to take place. Often, first drafts reflect the mood of the writer: the desire to simply get ideas on paper in an effort to solidify them, to make them real. First drafts are important because they are the beginning of the writing process. They should be an attempt to simply say, to allow thoughts to flow on paper without much attention to organization, transition, or strategy. Attention to the details of organization, transition, and strategy should occur after the initial ideas have been collected and transcribed onto the page.

Consider Structure and Organization as the Second Step to the Writing Process

Once ideas have been collected, stop and consider how you want them to be reflected. Paragraphs are developed using a number of strategies; which strategy will be most useful is inherent in your choice of topic sentence. Many different varieties of organization exist: comparison, contrast, definition, illustration, cause, effect. Choices for which organizational structure any writer decides on depend, to a degree, on context, overall goal of the essay, audience expectations, and, naturally, topic sentence.

A brief overview of the basic meaning of these varieties appears below.

Comparison

A comparison involves comparing two or more topics, ideas, themes, or points. Comparisons ask that the writer present information that shows how two or more points are similar in nature. Remember that you must have the same number of comments or points for each of the issues under comparison. You should not choose a topic if you know you have more to say about one of the two points than about the other. Comparisons should compare equally, or relatively so. In fact, if comparisons are not written exactly equally, it is often because the writer has decided to strategically use one of the topics to illuminate the other. To help you discover whether you have enough to say about any given topics, always consider them from the perspective of what is unexpected or unknown rather than expected. So, if you believe that U.S. president Barack Obama's speech on race was a fabulous model for the study of rhetoric, what can you say to oppose that belief? Once you have made some comments, ask yourself, "So what?"—as we did earlier in the book.

Contrast

A contrast involves contrasting two or more topics, ideas, themes, or points. Contrasts ask that the writer present information that shows how two or more points are different in nature. As is the case with comparisons, above, make sure that the items, theme, topics, and propositions you are contrasting are of more or less equal standing and that they are analytical in nature. That is, they are not simply a list of differences, but those differences are considered from a key standpoint. Hence, aim to argue about a key contrast between two or more things and then try to convince the reader that this "difference" amid essentially similar ideas is important. In order to show that you have considered your subject matter thoroughly, always aim to write about something that is not self-evident. Contrasts can be very effective, and they can show great analytical thought if—and only if—you work toward some larger key difference or point out a difference or two that is important but that the reader may not think of immediately. One could very well compare apples and oranges, since there are significant differences in flavour, texture, colour, and price—but of course they are both fruits, so all of this is obvious. Perhaps a paragraph on their aerodynamic properties and how splatter patterns determine which one gives better negative commentary to a poor production of Shakespeare would be more enlightening.

Cause

Cause paragraphs support the topic sentence by discussing the causes or reasons of something. Essentially, they endeavour to answer the question "What caused something or how did it become something?" Writers who consider using the cause format for organization must decide whether they will focus on only one major reason, developing it fully with a number of examples, or whether they will focus on a number of related reasons. Sometimes, a writer may choose to develop the cause paragraph by also introducing an alternative point of view, one that may not be as obvious or which may present or allow for the development of other paragraphs that further the initial thesis statement of the essay itself.

Effect

Effect is handled much the same way as is cause, except that effect paragraphs ask the writer to consider the consequences of something. As is the case with cause paragraphs, effect paragraphs may deal with only one major consequence or with many smaller ones.

Cause-and-effect paragraphs may be developed as individual paragraphs, or, as is the case with many topics, both causes (the reasons why something is something) and effects (the consequences of something) may be used in a single paragraph. In other words, sometimes a topic sentence may require that the writer deal with both the reasons for and the consequences of the topic itself. Often when this is the case, the cause or reason for the topic of the paragraph gives rise to the effects or consequences—a chain is created where A gives rise to B, B moves on to C, and so on. For example, the world fears the rise of the United States as a world power once again, even with President Obama at its helm. A topic like this would need to be supported with a number of believable reasons why the world would feel this way and the possible consequences of what the world would be like if in fact the United States bounced back from its current political, ideological, and economic state to once again be in a position of unipolar dominance. Causal relationships can be very complex, however, so when you are writing causal paragraphs, be very careful about what you label as a cause or an effect because you can be assured that your professor will take a very hard look at your logic.

Consider Patterns of Development

Sometimes writers just know how to present the information in their paragraph; sometimes organization is automatic and natural. When organization is not something that comes naturally during the writing process, it is necessary to give some consideration to the organization of the paragraph—the development of what you want to say and how you intend to say it. The following suggestions and patterns offer some basic guidelines.

Climatic Order

What comes first and what follows is something that should be strategically remembered. Going with the old saying "Put the weakest point in the middle" is not often good judgment. In fact, we recommend that all the examples used in the paragraph be strong. With this in mind, the following strategy seems to be best: begin the paragraph with a strong point that quickly, sufficiently, and expertly begins explaining, illustrating, qualifying, or defending your topic sentence. Traditional climatic order recommends moving from the least important point to the most important point. Although we agree with the basic premise underlying this method, we suggest a slight alteration to the original plan: leave the second strongest point for the very end. People always remember what they read last, and going with the second strongest point at the end assures that your strongest ideas are equally represented. The strongest point solidifies and guarantees audience participation in the reading process; it serves to show that your topic sentence can be developed in an interesting way. The final point is strong enough to make the reader nod his or her head in agreement and to encourage him or her to move on. Keep the other points for the middle of the paragraph. These should serve to either elaborate or extend the points that came before, or to enhance some idea. Use transitions wisely to help move the paragraph along in a coherent and swift fashion.

Inductive Order

This order is used fairly infrequently in the academic model, and rarely as the first or last paragraph of a formal academic essay. The inductive order is fairly popular in that it begins with a fairly interesting but general main idea that is then supported with various examples that back up the main idea of interest found in the first sentence. The last sentence sums up the preceding information using an inductive inference (a general principle arrived at logically, through analysis of the specific examples) that ties back to the topic sentence.

Deductive Order

This order is more common in the academic paper. The deductive order requires that the first sentence of the paragraph be the general topic sentence and that the remaining sentences provide sufficient proof or backings to support the general topic sentence. This model is usually taught in university writing centres as the "inverted pyramid" model (think of an upside-down pyramid) because it begins with a general topic and progressively becomes

---

BOX 3.2 | **EXAMPLE OF AN ALTERNATION PATTERN PARAGRAPH**

General Topic Sentence:
Some primates have demonstrated that they may be capable of understanding basic grammar.

Point 1A:
For example, language enculturated apes have been shown to have basic understanding of differences in syntax.

Point 1B (either compared to A or contrasted):
However, this understanding has not convincingly included recursion, which many linguists believe is the hallmark of human language.

Point 2A:
Kanzi, a bonobo at Great Ape Trust, did outperform a human child in a series of language tasks (Savage-Rumbaugh et al. 3[7]).

Point 2B (either compared to A or contrasted):
In comparison, no other apes have been documented in matching his achievement.

Point 3A:
Many monkeys in the wild do have distinct calls for different predators.

Point 3B (either compared to A or contrasted):
Nevertheless, there is no proof that these calls contain what we would call grammar.

Note that the points are often connected with the appropriate transition words: *although, moreover, further, in comparison, in contrast, likewise, subsequently, and so, also, like,* etc.

---

more specific, until it ends with a point. Usually, writers attempt to provide a very strong first example, followed by an example to the example (i.e., further clarification to the example, one that points to something very specific) and then a number of other examples that work to enhance, elaborate, and extend upon the idea presented in the general topic sentence. These paragraphs in the academic essay are generally quite long and detailed, and their purpose is to deductively persuade the reader to accept a proposition or main claim.

Block Pattern

The block pattern is used when writing either a comparison or a contrast paper. Block pattern refers to the organization or structure of the information in either the comparison or contrast. In the block pattern, writers typically divide the topic into two parts. They devote one entire paragraph to one side and then they either compare or contrast in the other paragraph. This way of presenting information can be very effective if the writer remembers to deal with both sides equally and if the writer does not rearrange the order of the points being compared or contrasted.

Alternation Patterns

These are also common means of organizing comparison or contrast papers. Instead of dealing with one topic at a time, the alternation pattern deals with one point at a time. Each point is then either compared or contrasted.

SPECIAL CONSIDERATION: SPICING UP YOUR PARAGRAPHS

Most writers adopt a sentence style and stick to it. Although there is nothing wrong with sticking to a good thing, readers really do appreciate some variety to help the reading process along. But while writers of the academic essay can use various transition words to connect ideas between sentences and using synonyms and antonyms, metaphor and illustration to provide various examples as support, they can also vary their sentence style strategically to highlight some points and downplay others. Here are a few tips:

1. **Vary sentence length.** If you tend to write long sentences combined with a number of semi-colons and transition words, consider shortening your sentences periodically to break up the monotony of the reading process and to draw the reader's attention to a key point.

2. **Consider what the key sentence to your paragraph is.** Often, the key sentence is manifested through the best idea, or the best example, that a writer can come up with. Sometimes, the key sentence appears as an analytical discussion of a number of examples that came before. Once you have figured out what the key sentence is, look at the remaining sentences in your paragraph. If your sentences are short, consider making the key sentence a longer one. Consider combining one or two ideas into subordinate and independent sentences to make both a physical and a semantic connection for the reader. If your sentences are long, break the key sentence up strategically. Punctuation is a very powerful rhetorical tool. It draws the attention of the reader's eye as well as his breath. Strategic punctuation, as long as it is grammatically correct, can physically force a reader to slow his or her reading pace and therefore focus on the key idea.

3. **Consider adding some parallel sentences for dramatic effect.** Parallel sentences are useful because they force the reader to see how ideas are hierarchically similar in nature. Often, writers list points in groups of threes (sometimes more); these lists are parallel in sentence structure, and they encourage a type of flow and rhythm that would not usually be gained with a traditional sentence style. See Chapter 8 for some pointers.

4. **Consider creating a periodic sentence to build up dramatically to the main idea.** Periodic sentences begin with a subordinate idea that is then developed through the main clause. Periodic sentences can be quite long and intricate; they can have more than one subordinate clause, which then makes its way toward the main clause for the ultimate

effect. Consider creating a loose sentence to strategically draw the reader's attention to the main idea and then reinforce the validity of that idea through the use of subordinate clauses that offer support to that main idea. Loose sentences are a good way to offer an informal tone to a formal piece of text; used effectively, they display a writer's prowess in that they allow a writer to put first things first and then elaborate as necessary for clarity and strategy.

Varying sentence style helps writers achieve what they want to accomplish with the paragraph, but the words that you use to compose your sentences are just as important as the overall ideas presented in the paragraphs themselves. Remember, too, that you can always infuse variety into your sentences by re-examining them and simply considering how to say something differently. For example, if you tend to use the verb *to be* (or a form of it, such as *was* or *is*) a lot in your writing, consider changing to a more dynamic verb type. The verb *to be* in its varying forms is easy to use and encourages writers to create sentences that are habitually wordy, static, and passive. Whenever possible, eliminate unnecessary uses of the verb *to be* and replace them with more dynamic verbs that emphasize action. Ask yourself, "What is the goal of the sentence? What is the subject trying to accomplish?" and then replace the typical copular (connecting, existing) verb with something more dynamic. Doing so will often require that you restructure the presentation of your subject as well. Compare "Blogging is something that you do in private but it has public consequences" to "Bloggers engage in public communication from the private realm."

GRAMMAR **TIP**

The use of active verbs will make your writing more "lively."

Example: "It is known that traditional grammar is preferred by many monkeys" versus "Research shows that many monkeys prefer traditional grammar."

Writing Body Paragraphs

THE CONCLUDING SENTENCE

Fortunately, good paragraph endings, although important, are not the be-all and end-all of a great essay (although a great conclusion is). Nevertheless, a paragraph has to have an end. Often, the end comes naturally; writers simply know when their thoughts are complete. Sometimes, however, the end is not so natural, and we have to stop and think about when enough is enough. Here are some tips to help you create a good ending when it seems that none are in sight.

- Consider an ending that helps the paragraph come full circle—one that points back to the topic sentence somehow and in this way draws the paragraph to a close.

- Without saying "in conclusion" (because we reserve this for conclusions proper—if that!), consider letting the ideas taper off naturally. Ask yourself whether you have provided the necessary three major examples and three minor examples to your topic sentence. And if you have, try to end with a comment that foreshadows the next idea.

- Consider presenting your final example in a stylistically interesting way. If you have written the entire paragraph using short informative sentences, why not combine one or two into a longer sentence? *Compound* and *complex* sentences not only draw the reader's eye to the physical difference on the page, but they also encourage the reader to read differently. If you do go this route, make sure that your final sentence is your best example for that particular topic and remember to not use this method for all paragraphs or it will take away from the stylistic and strategic effect.

- The purpose of each paragraph is to support and develop the main idea: the concluding sentence of a paragraph should relate the purpose of the paragraph (expressed in the topic sentence) to the purpose of the essay. This is particularly important if the paragraph provides evidence that directly supports your claim. Do not assume that your professor sees the connection. In fact, tying paragraphs back to your main claim, and even sometimes explicitly to your thesis statement, is a great way to avoid digression and ensure that you remain cohesive.

If you are one of those writers who tends to write more, not less, and have long-winded paragraphs, ask yourself how much information is really necessary and carefully consider what you have written with respect to your thesis statement and the overall goals of your essay. It is very important to remember that, although there may be a wealth of information surrounding your particular topic, only the very best information should actually make its way into your essay. What goes in must be of direct and specific relevance to the thesis statement.

NOTES

1. De Waal, Frans. "Bonobo Sex and Society: The Behaviour of a Close Relative Challenges Assumptions About Male Supremacy in Human Evolution." *Scientific American* Mar. 1995: 82–88. Print.

2. Kaplan, Matt (2008). "'Loving' Bonobos Seen Killing, Eating Other Primates." |*National Geographic News.* National Geographic Society, 13 Oct. 2008. Web. 5 April 2011. <http://news.nationalgeographic.com/news/2008/10/081013-bonobos-attack-missions.html>.

3. Van Dijk, Margaret. *Basics and Beyond: Paragraphs and Essay Strategies.* Toronto: Pearson, 2002. Print.

4. Kane, Thomas, and Heather Pyrcz. *The Canadian Oxford Guide to Writing: A Rhetoric and Handbook*, 2nd ed. Don Mills, ON: Oxford University Press, 2008. Print.

5. Halliday, M.A.K., and C.M.I.M. Matthiessen. *An Introduction to Functional Grammar*, 3rd ed. London: Arnold, 2004. Print.

6. Examples adapted from Martin, James. *English Text: System and Structure.* Philadelphia: John Benjamins, 1992. Print.

7. Savage-Rumbaugh, Sue, et al. "Language Comprehension in Ape and Child." Monographs of the Society for Research in Child Development 233.58. Chicago: University of Chicago Press, 1993. Print.

So, What Is My Thesis?
Creating a Valid and Valuable Argument

HOW TO APPROACH A TOPIC CRITICALLY

There are several levels of critical response, and not all of them are considered equal. Assuming that your writing is mechanically sound (and if it isn't, see Chapter 8!), your mark will largely depend on how "deep" your argument goes. The problem is that most teachers do not really explain what it means to have an approach with some depth.

In essence, the issue once again boils down to personal taste and the reality that not every writer's style will agree with every reader. Nevertheless, some strategies and considerations exist to help you present your position in an objective and academically effective way.

First, analytical thought is usually objective in nature. The best way to show objectivity is to avoid the use of the first person pronouns—namely *I*. For most students, the fundamental conflict (presenting a subjective opinion objectively) inherent in this reality presents a dilemma because the writer's point of view is ultimately personal and value-laden and the position is usually one that the writer can (most willingly) support! So why avoid the pronoun *I*?

Ultimately, the answer is quite simple—if perhaps not pleasant: if everything in the essay is about you, generally, you probably have a very shallow level of critical engagement. In other words, writers engage with the text when they move away from their own positions (the value of like or dislike that we might place on something) toward looking at the topic from a different light—how interesting, exciting, important, compelling something is (and why) rather than whether or not you like or disliked it. This chapter is designed to show you a number of different approaches to your argument that are more likely to get you that A grade than "I don't like Hamlet because he is a weenie."

DIFFERENT APPROACHES TO ARGUMENT

Just because we say that you shouldn't have as your thesis "I like this book because ... " doesn't mean that you will not be led by this reaction—you just shouldn't stop there! By all means, start with material that gives you an emotional reaction. The best writing usually comes from reactions to something that is inspiring or enraging, and those reactions are often vital in compelling you to move from having a topic to taking a stance on it.

You must, however, take your reaction to the next level of analysis and craft your argument accordingly. So let's say that you are a big fan of hip-hop and rap. You've been given an assignment where you are expected to "engage with an example of popular culture." You're excited that you finally have a chance to connect a first love of gangsta rap with a second love of essay writing (right?). In looking at the history of the genre, you decide to get old school and talk about the roots of this musical form as embodied in N.W.A.'s seminal 1988 album, *Straight Outta Compton.*

How do you go about connecting the fact that you really like this album with the critical response that the professor is expecting? Certainly, if you simply make the argument "I like this music," you will not do very well. Even if you expand your thesis to "I like this album because it is great party music, it makes me feel good, and it really rocks," you will at best get a pat on the head and a pity mark. The reason is simple: all of these points are completely subjective (in other words, they all relate to an individual and his or her emotional responses). While undoubtedly true, the arguments do not pass the "Who cares?" test—because the only honest answer is "You" (and maybe a couple of your friends). Essentially, when you go to expand these arguments, you will be hard-pressed to integrate expert sources, and we all know that your professors are expecting some sort of bibliographical references. People who study educational objectives call these types of emotional approaches "affective," and even when they are done very well they tend to be less valued than more "cognitive" approaches. Simply, your professors want you to react less with your gut and more with your noggin.

Moving from Subjective to Objective Analysis

So how do we move from subjective to objective analysis? First of all, follow that advice of your high school English teachers: get rid of the *I*. Even though it is perfectly true that all of your arguments are going to come from you, it is equally true that the reader doesn't need to be reminded of that. Also, if you rephrase your basic argument to pull out the *I*, the supporting arguments and evidence will be chosen more judiciously to support the more objective approach. For example, let's rephrase your main point away from the "I like" approach, and more into the "assertion of value" approach. So, your thesis evolves into something like "The N.W.A. album *Straight Outta Compton* is a vital contribution to the rap genre." Instead of focusing on the personal here, the paper applies your understanding of the music into the greater realm of musical knowledge. As such, the supporting points will undoubtedly be more in line with accepted modes of academic proof.

There are, in fact, various *types* of cognitive activity, as epitomized in the essay. We all remember the book report genre from

1. Knowledge

2. Comprehension

3. Application

4. Analysis

5. Synthesis

6. Evaluation

Source: Bloom, Benjamin S. *Taxonomy of Educational Objectives Book 1/ Cognitive Domain, 1st Edition,* © 1984. Printed and Electronically reproduced by permission of Pearson Education, Inc., Upper Saddle River, New Jersey.

grade school: what you are proving at this level is that you have read the book and understand basically what has happened (in other words, a "plot summary"). Such an exercise reflects the first level of academic engagement, in that all you are proving is that you "know" the text in question. Have a look at "Bloom's Taxonomy" (Benjamin Bloom and his psychologist colleagues put this together in 1956),[1] and most educators are at least familiar with it or else apply it subconsciously to their marking criteria.

Each of the categories in "Bloom's Taxonomy" is associated with certain process types, and these process types describe the kinds of actions you would take for that sort of cognitive activity:

1. *Knowledge:* to arrange, to count, to define, to describe, to draw, to duplicate, to find, to identify, to label, to list, to match, to memorize, to name, to quote, to recognize, to recall, to recite, to reproduce. Essentially, this category is just about remembering stuff and spitting it back out. For example: there is a robot made out of Lego.

2. *Comprehension:* to classify, to conclude, to demonstrate, to describe, to discuss, to explain, to generalize, to identify, to illustrate, to interpret, to locate, to paraphrase, to predict, to report, to restate, to review, to select, to translate.

The category of comprehension adds in a sort of meaning that you must grasp and demonstrate knowledge of: why someone would make a robot out of Lego.

3. *Application:* to change, to choose, to compute, to demonstrate, to dramatize, to employ, to illustrate, to interview, to operate, to practice, to prepare, to produce, to select, to solve, to transfer, to use. Application is about taking the original material and using it in new situations according to patterns, rules, or laws; for example, what makes that particular configuration robotlike?

4. *Analysis:* to appraise, to calculate, to categorize, to characterize, to compare and contrast, to criticize, to debate, to deduce, to differentiate, to examine, to outline, to question, to relate, to separate, to test. Analysis is about taking something apart along structural lines to reveal that structure. If you smash your Lego robot, you'll note that you are left with individual blocks. What is their nature?

5. *Synthesis:* to arrange, to collect, to compose, to construct, to create, to design, to develop, to formulate, to integrate, to invent, to make, to perform, to plan, to prepare, to propose, to rewrite. Synthesis takes over where analysis leaves off, and puts stuff back together, but this time to construct a new whole. So, given two different Lego robots, how might we amalgamate their blocks into some kind of mega-robot?

6. *Evaluation:* to appraise, to argue, to assess, to choose, to compare, to conclude, to critique, to decide, to defend, to estimate, to judge, to justify, to predict, to prioritize, to prove, to rank, to select, to value. Evaluation is all about judging the effectiveness of material for a given purpose, based on set criteria. For example, how effective a robot that is made from Lego may be, according to the criteria of size, mobility, and attack effectiveness (I'm assuming, of course, that you wish your Lego robot to take over the world, not to vacuum your carpet!)

One thing that you'll note is that each of these categories assumes the mastery of the category underneath it—and in fact, when illustrating these levels, most texts choose to use a pyramid where "knowledge" is at the bottom and "evaluation" is at the top. The theory is that if you are able to evaluate, you are able to do all of the other tasks underneath it: so the problem is that if you are only demonstrating knowledge, the professor can't be sure that you are in fact capable of higher types of cognitive activity, and assesses you accordingly.

APPLYING OBJECTIVE ANALYSIS TO ANSWER THE QUESTION "WHAT DOES MY PROFESSOR WANT *ME* TO DO?"

There are, of course, many different types of assignment. Some professors will provide you with an argument, in which case you can skip to the next section. However, most professors aren't going to be that easy on you. They tend to supply you with a topic, and then you have to take that topic and come up with the approach that best suits that level of analysis. In fact, even if the essay is an exercise in demonstrating knowledge (your ability to reiterate what it was that you learned in the year), it helps to have a grasp of the different levels of assessment most often used. If your professor provides you with a synthesis of material from different texts, you are expected to (a) be familiar with the various texts and (b) be able to follow and demonstrate the synthesis between them. You'll have a much better chance of that if indeed you are able to understand the synthesis process type described above, or better yet, carry it out!

On the other hand, most assignments simply provide the primary sources, and in doing so suggest a means to approach them via the process types above. If we ask you to compare and contrast two texts, you are obviously going to be engaged in a synthesis activity, and so you should plan your writing for this task. (See the discussion of paragraph types in the last chapter for an idea of how to structure these arguments.) If we ask you to "examine" a single text, your task is one of analysis, so we are really asking you how the text *functions* as an example of its type, and what it is about that text that makes it function in that way.

A good approach is to actually pick out the process words on your assignment sheet and cross-reference them with the list above. Then, once you know the type of task you are expected to perform, you can write out an argument straight from other items on that list, using similar process types. In the above example of N.W.A.'s *Straight Outta Compton* exercise, you were given the rather generic process of "engage." Since there are many types of engagement, you are a bit freer in choosing which type your essay should centre on. The prior choice, to assert that the album is a vital contribution to the rap genre, is along the lines of an "analysis" (although being rather vague, it could easily shift into evaluative. In fact, an evaluative approach may be an even better choice, assuming that you have enough understanding of the genre and its position in the history of music to make such evaluation worthwhile). Since we know from "Bloom's Taxonomy" that analysis is all about constituent parts, you could take various elements of the album to use as part of your proof. First, that several members of N.W.A. (notably Eazy-E, Dr. Dre, and Ice Cube) went on to very successful solo careers, thus affirming their talent. Second, that the choice to use explicit lyrics proved that it was possible to gain a following despite a lack of radio play simply by accurately reflecting the language of the streets. Finally, that because this language accurately reflected the situation in their neighbourhood (i.e., Compton, California), the album became a vital form of social commentary.

GRAMMAR **TIP** : WHO VS. WHOM

In essence, *who* is the one doing stuff, and *whom* is getting it done to him or her. "Who stole my grammar book?" "It was the monkey who did it." "To whom should I complain?"

ERRORS IN ARGUMENT: AN EXAMINATION OF COMMON LOGICAL FALLACIES

Typically, putting together an argument isn't that difficult. At least, it isn't that hard to convince people who don't need a lot of convincing (for example, a drunken friend is highly prone to the suggestion that he or she should drink more). The problem is that your professor has seen a lot of argument structure, and some is simply weak—or downright wrong!

The ancient study of rhetoric is about putting together convincing arguments, and Aristotle's *Rhetoric*[2] (written around 350 BCE) is still in use today as one of the best sources for types of appeal. To put it simply, he said that you could convince in one of three ways: through the character of the speaker (*ethos*), the emotional state of the hearer (*pathos*), or the logic of the argument itself (*logos*). It is also possible to make an argument that is couched in humour, which can probably be seen as a subset of *pathos* but is also referred to as *comos*. There is really no such thing as an argument that is solely any one of these categories, but most texts are designed to rely on one to a greater degree than the others.

Imagine, for example, one of those ads depicting some guy in a lab coat with a stethoscope around his neck. You assume he is a doctor, and so obviously the commercial is arguing from a position of authority in which we assume his intelligence, virtue, and goodwill. Now let's say that he looks at the camera and tells us, "If you don't use this medicine, you will die a slow, horrible death." Here there are actually two different types of appeal. There is a basic kind of logic (If not A, then B will result), and there is an appeal to the emotional state of the presumed audience: fear of death will ensure that you take advantage of the product.

The problem in the above example is that we can also reject these appeals. We know he is not really a doctor, so the appeal to *ethos* is not very strong, especially if we don't believe being an actor presumes exceptionally high intelligence, an exceptional sense of virtue, or a particularly strong goodwill. We can also reject the basic logical premise, since we have not yet suffered a slow and horrible death, despite not using the medication being recommended. And of course, the appeal to fear only works if we are already in a fearful state, so that hypochondriacs might find this commercial convincing, but those in reasonable mental and physical health would undoubtedly ignore it. However, if the commercial is really, really campy (in other words, so over the top that we couldn't take it seriously anyway) then it might have the appeal to our sense of humour, which may or may not lead us to purchasing the product, but at the least would provide a chance for the appeal to take place.

The long and short, though, is that different appeals work in different situations for different reasons. Apparently, contemporary politics is mostly built on an appeal to emotions, rather than anything logical, but it is also premised on the voting public somehow trusting the politicians who are putting forth the appeals as being strangely superior to the average person—a trust that doesn't seem to be supported by the facts! Your job, though, is to create the type of appeal that is going to be most convincing in an academic setting, and that appeal is predominantly *logos*: your professors want some sort of logical argument underpinning your paper. Many people mistake this preference for academic writing being "boring"—and we admit it, much of academic writing *is* boring!—but just because you must have a sound underlying argument does not mean that you cannot also have interesting writing.

One very basic problem, though, is that all of us are surrounded by crappy arguments. The person trying to sell us cologne on TV is exploiting the needs, values, and lifestyles of the audience that specific advertisement is geared toward, by making it seem like the scent does the trick. The woman with the perfect skin in the magazine is trying to make us believe that some product she's never actually used is responsible for her genetically endowed epidermis. News shows try to scare us by hyping sensational crime as a common occurrence in our neighbourhoods, and pop songs sell us a vision of a world in which everyone is rich and young and in love. All of these types of text have obvious appeals, but none of them would be very good to hand in as an essay.

Here, then, is a list of the most common logical problems that student writing suffers from (and we bet you will find a lot of other texts suffering from them as well!). You've probably heard some of these in the context of having arguments with someone, and in fact that is where most of them derive from—the art of debating. If you are familiar with these logical problems, you have the choice: you can either avoid them, or you can exploit them. We would suggest that you do both. Avoid them on your essays, since most professors will dismiss a paper that is reliant on these types of error, but exploit them with your friends in order to win arguments (okay, we can't really recommend the latter. Use your rhetorical powers only for good!).

1. Has your mother ever accused you of *Begging the Question*? Essentially, this means that you are arguing something is true by simply asserting that it is true—often just using different words. In its most extreme form, Begging the Question is a circular argument, something akin to "Love is the feeling you get when you are in love." If you are assuming an underlying reality that is not necessarily shared with the reader, you risk alienating that reader. Begging the Question is also related to a *semantic argument*.

2. *The Black and White World* is a place where only two options are possible—you are *either* with us *or* you are with the terrorists (at least, according to the argument of former U.S. president George W. Bush). Such a worldview ignores the richness of possibility and also risks rejection from anyone who does not share such a stark version of reality or who has a more multifaceted view on events. This approach boils down to oversimplification and often relies on an emotional argument to convince audience acceptance—and is particularly poor in an academic paper, where nuance is a much better approach.

3. *Correlation* is the statistical likelihood that two events will occur at the same time or in the presence of each other, or even one after the other. *Causality* is when one event actively leads to another because the first event took place. Correlation and causality are not the same thing: it is perfectly possible for events to share a statistical likelihood of occurring (perhaps based on a third, unknown, factor) and yet one does not cause the other. The entire Church of the Flying Spaghetti Monster is (deliberately) based on this fallacy: adherents dress as pirates for religious occasions because there is a strong inverse correlation between average global temperatures and the number of pirates in the world. In other words, as the number of pirates has decreased worldwide, the average global temperature has risen. In order to combat global warming, then, Church of the Flying Spaghetti Monster adherents try to fool the global climate by looking like pirates, in order to offset the lack of real pirates. Vengaza.org even has a handy chart to prove its assertion (see page 86).

4. The *False Analogy* is when a writer makes a comparison between two things in order to draw a similar conclusion in both cases. For example, animal rights activists' claim that "meat is murder" is based on an equivocation between animals and human beings, since *murder* as a legal term is premised on the fact that a human is being killed. In order to accept the argument that the production of meat for human consumption is an example of murder, we must accept that

FIGURE 4-1

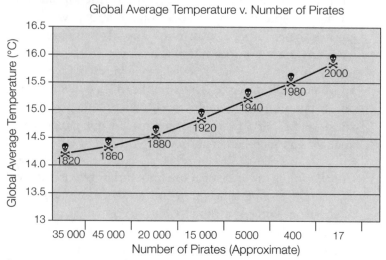

Global Average Temperature v. Number of Pirates

Source: Venganza. Found at: http://www.venganza.org/about/open-letter/.

the animals being slaughtered for meat are deserving of the same rights as humans (which is the actual debatable point!). Academic arguments often deal with classifications, and even subtle differences between terms are often very important. Making equivocations such as "meat is murder" won't work in an academic context unless you can make a case from an objective point of view that acknowledges and respects the opposing point of view. False analogies often begin with categorical statements such as "meat is murder" that ignore distinctions important to others. Always be aware of the opposing point of view. For comparison to the "meat is murder" false analogy, consider this rebuttal: if all consumption of carbon-based life forms is a type of murder, then the division between humans and other animals is just as arbitrary as the one between animals and plants. Thus, none of us should eat anything organic, and within a month or so there will be no one left to make any sort of argument. Can you spot the equivocation?

5. Perhaps the most fun logical fallacy is the *Personal Attack* (or ad hominem attack, which literally means "against

the man"—somewhat different than "sticking it to the man," though). Essentially what it means is, if you know that you can't win an argument, you just start calling the other person names. Watching an entertainer such as Fox News Channel's Bill O'Reilly calling people Nazis or far-left loons will give you a good idea of how people supplement a poor or non-existent argument with name-calling. One advantage of this approach is that while an audience will rarely consider you either correct or ethical for name-calling, you may anger your opponent into dealing with the attack instead of the substance of the argument, and in doing so make him or her lose the overall debate.

6. Producing a *Semantic Argument*, also known as equivocating, is a technique whereby you play around with word meaning instead of dealing with content. Perhaps you have been in a disagreement where the other person claims that you are relying on semantics—basically, that you are relying on a different definition of a word than that of most people. Former U.S. president Bill Clinton famously stated about his intern, Monika Lewinsky, "I did not have sexual relations with that woman." However, the lurid details of the relationship that thereafter became public knowledge forced Clinton to reveal his semantic argument: he claimed that he believed the commonly accepted definition of "sexual relations" did not include the category of oral sex. (Clinton also famously stated before a U.S. Grand Jury, "It depends on what the meaning of the word 'is' is," a statement that make some sense in context but was greatly ridiculed as a semantic argument when taken out of it.)

7. A *Slippery Slope* argument is an argument toward causality that in actual fact is unlikely to be true. Perhaps the most famed example of this is the argument from the "war on drugs," whereby so-called soft drugs are considered gateways into more dangerous drugs. In fact, this argument stems from a confusion of correlation and causation: many serious drug abusers did indeed use alcohol, tobacco, or cannabis at an earlier time. However, studies found that the predictability of moving from cannabis into drugs such as

heroin is difficult to ascertain, and that the probability of one type of drug use leading into another is quite low. As another example, let's say that there is a strong correlation between lack of adequate sleep and committing murder, and we know that caffeine causes a stimulant effect that makes sleep more elusive. Just because 98.6 percent of murderers in North America had coffee in the year prior to committing murder does not mean that the use of coffee will eventually lead to murder! (Note that all numerical assertions in the previous argument are also pure invention.)

8. A *Sob Story* is simply an argument predicated on inducing an emotional state in the listener, typically to arouse sympathy. Certainly, a decent sob story may be enough to convince someone to give you bus fare, but it will almost never be enough to get you an A, so it is best avoided as the core to an argument.

9. A common rhetorical technique, but one that is no more valid for being common, is the *Straw Man Argument*. Essentially, instead of debating your opponent, you construct a false or exaggerated argument (the "straw man") that you proceed to attack. For example, let's say that your partner has decided you should stop leaving your dirty socks on the kitchen table, and for some odd reason you wish to continue this behaviour. If your counter-argument is along the lines of "What you are essentially saying is that I should buy a new set of socks every day! How absurd!" then you are first misrepresenting your partner's argument and then dismissing it. And while you might enrage your partner enough to shift the argument to other ground, to an outside observer you will not be the victor. Related is the "red herring" technique—which means bringing up a point that is not relevant at all in order to distract the opponent or reader. While misdirection is the core of the magician's game, it is not particularly valued in an academic paper.

10. Finally, you can make the mistake of not understanding *Whose Burden of Proof* it is. It is up to those asserting something to provide evidence in support of that assertion.

The difficulty lies when something is not properly supported by the evidence (or misrepresented as being proven when it is not!). Further, there is the problem of slanting, which is providing only that evidence that supports your assertion and ignoring all other types of evidence that might contradict it. Remember, in judo as in academics, it is sometimes wisest to make the opponent's strength into a weakness. At the crux of this fallacy is the difficulty of proving a negative assertion. One well-known example is the assertion that God exists because it is impossible to prove that God does not exist. When you are making an academic argument, the burden of proof is always on you, and not your audience.

Avoiding these errors in argument is quite important to constructing a solid thesis and supporting proof. The final piece of the puzzle is integrating your research into the argument structure, and so the next chapter will turn to this concern.

NOTES

1. Bloom, B. S., M.D. Engelhart, E.J. Furst, W.H. Hill, and D.R. Krathwoh. *Taxonomy of Educational Objectives: The Classification of Educational Goals: Handbook I: Cognitive Domain.* New York: Longmans, Green, 1956. Print.

2. Aristotle. *Rhetoric.* Trans. W. Rys Roberts. *The Internet Classics Archive.* Web Atomics and Massachusetts Institute of Technology, n.d. Web. 5 April 2011. <http://classics.mit.edu/Aristotle/rhetoric.html>.

CHAPTER 5

Organizing the Discussion

The "Thinking Body" of Your Essay

THE BIG PICTURE: USING ORGANIZATION TO MAKE YOUR POINT

Linking Paragraphs to a Purpose

Earlier, we examined some of the mechanics involved in writing individual body paragraphs, from the topic sentence, through the development, to the conclusion. But in essays, paragraphs are not written in isolation: they are the building blocks of the essay, and they must have that quality called organization, which means both that they occur in a sensible order and that they work together as a whole. This chapter will examine how to harmonize the body paragraphs with your introduction and conclusion, and it will provide several strategies for better organizing your essays. To extend the building blocks analogy a little further, the focus of this chapter may be compared to both the mortar that binds those bricks together and the plan required to put the bricks together in the first place. This chapter will introduce a sophisticated plan that gives each paragraph a specific function in your essay. Once you can write with a plan, your body paragraphs will be linked to your purpose, and your essays will attain levels of organization and clarity that will surely impress your professors.

The Introduction and Conclusion Frame the Body

If the introduction and conclusion of your essay are where you frame, declare, and sum up your argument, then the discussion section—the body of your essay—is where you actually develop your ideas and prove your thesis through argument, illustration, and analysis. The discussion section is where effective essays realize the full potential of their theses and where the truly great essays pack every paragraph with proofs and new insights, all of which clearly and strategically develop the significance and validity of their arguments. Without a great body, a good thesis is no more than an empty promise or an excellent start to a race—because even after crafting a bold and thought-provoking opening, you must still keep your promise or finish the race. Even Albert Einstein's theory of relativity would not have been accepted without his discussion, in which he developed his ideas and proved his theory using illustrations and down-to-earth examples, all the while building upon scholarly knowledge, modifying and adapting the theories of others to explain his own. In fact, the very same techniques he used to prove his theory of relativity are available for you to develop and prove your ideas. So, although there are various nuts and bolts to writing effective discussions— we will discuss them shortly—the number-one priority of every effective discussion is to realize the full potential of its thesis.

CONSIDER A TRADITIONAL APPROACH

Instruction regarding essay bodies is remarkably sparse, especially when you consider that the discussion section is by far the largest section of most essays. Even in a five-paragraph essay, the middle paragraphs constitute 60 percent of the essay, and in the 2000-plus word research essays you will write for upper-year courses, that proportion could exceed 90 percent. Many students report, however, that in their high-school English classes, the only instruction they received about writing essay bodies was something along these lines:

- Provide at least three points that support your thesis.

- Provide examples—ideally three—to prove each point.

- Take one paragraph—at the most, two—to develop each point.

- Make sure that each paragraph follows a consistent, parallel form. For example, the five-sentence paragraph would have a point, then three examples, then a concluding sentence tying the examples to the point and, preferably, back to the thesis.

We should begin by saying that, even though this advice is geared particularly toward five-paragraph essays written on general topics in non-academic settings, it is still good advice. Many university-level students would be well served by this advice, and students who have the most problems writing undergraduate essays typically never received—or else never heeded—those suggestions.

The University Paper

Although every high-school graduate entering university has written essays, it is common for first-year students—sometimes even those who have done relatively well in high-school English—to struggle with university-level essays. Why does this happen, and what is so different about university-level essays and evaluation? Are expectations simply higher in university, or have students have been inadequately instructed in writing fundamentals such as grammar and organization? The answer is a bit of both—but there is much more to the story. The truth is, in our experience, that most students enter university with some competence in writing personal narratives and organizing their writing both chronologically and topically. So, it is not that high schools do not teach writing, but that the modes of writing that students learn in high school do not explicitly prepare them to excel at university-level essays.

Specifically, a majority of first-year university students appear fairly comfortable producing these three kinds, or *genres*, of writing:

1. personal modes of expression where they are expressing their opinion or judgment of an issue to a non-judgmental audience;

2. the kind of straightforward description and communication of information used in both simple reports and reviews. Many students demonstrate some facility in communicating data in comprehensible prose, and some demonstrate fairly high proficiency in paragraphing and creative embellishment; and

3. narratives, both creative and non-creative, in which events are organized in chronological, cause-and-effect relationships.

However, most academic writing involves a completely different *audience*: not a sympathetic, non-judgmental audience but a knowledgeable and often demanding one that expects all relationships to be fully and clearly developed and all arguments to be proven through vigorous analysis, founded upon appropriate, cited research. As well, the most-taught modes of organization (chronological and cause–effect narratives) are often ineffective at structuring certain assignments, such as the critical analysis or the argumentative essay.

Understanding how to write for an academic audience is the key to succeeding at university-level essays. But the change in perspective is full of challenges because it involves a completely different way of thinking about your essay as a whole. Academic audiences are not unreasonable, but the high degree of organization and clarity they require may at first seem daunting and even unattainable. Your professors are trained to look for logical and factual inconsistencies, and they require that you organize your work using more than topical associations and transitional sentences. The very structure of your essay must facilitate your purpose, and to satisfy their expectations, you need a strategy for organizing your discussion. This chapter will outline a proven strategy for organizing academic essays that is based on logic and purpose. It is a simple strategy for treating the discussion section—both the section as a whole and each paragraph individually within it—as a logical extension and proof of your thesis. The focus on your thesis will provide all the clarity and coherence your audience demands. And the logical framework of the model developed by the British logician Stephen Toulmin in the 1950s[1] will ensure that each paragraph will have a productive purpose in the grand scheme of your essay. Simply by using this framework for writing your discussions, you will dramatically improve how academic audiences receive your papers.

HOW TO ORGANIZE YOUR PAPER AROUND AN ARGUMENT

The Toulmin Model: A Logical Approach to Organizing Your Essay

BOX 5.1

Monkeys like bananas.

Jessica likes bananas.

Therefore, Jessica is a monkey.

If you ever study formal logic, you will learn that this is an example of abused syllogism, and you will likely encounter an array of rules governing proposition, premises, and inferences, all of which are supposed to guarantee that logic and truth claims are logically airtight. The problem is, however, that most of the claims you will make and defend in your essays will be argued about issues about which there is no universal certainty, and although your arguments will be judged according to certain standards of logic and factual accuracy, most of your papers will address matters of interpretation and opinion, not indisputable matters of fact. Stephen Toulmin developed a useful model for describing and thinking about the kinds of arguments people make about arguable issues, and we will simplify and adapt the *Toulmin model* to the task of writing effective undergraduate essays. Though the model does concern logic, it is important to

FIGURE 5-1

The Toulmin Model

DATA

CLAIM

WARRANTS

REBUTTALS

QUALIFIERS

BACKING

understand that this logic is different from the formal logic you may encounter in philosophy. It is not about adhering to correct forms or deducing universal truths; it is about persuading a reasonable, informed audience.

As you can see, you need to learn only six words. But before we talk about how to structure essays around the Toulmin model, let's learn what the terms mean and how they map out the basic structure of any argument.

Data: What Your Thesis Is About

Data are the assumptions or facts that form the basis for your claim. For instance, if you will be making a claim about a particular issue (say, digital piracy), then your data will be the set of facts that prompt your claim. You should always be wary of treating assumptions as facts, but in many circumstances, depending upon your assignment and on your audience, you may treat another's debated theory as the starting point for your own exploratory argument. The general principle is that facts are not necessarily universal truths but rather arguments that have been proven, at least to the satisfaction of the writer and audience involved. In fact, in essays by more advanced writers, each reason (warrant) supporting the thesis is itself a claim requiring a whole argument to prove it before it can stand as a validating principle of the thesis. This method of building your core argument upon a series of smaller arguments, which in some cases may be supported by further arguments, is called *layered reasoning*, and it is a hallmark of sophisticated essays.

For example, let us imagine that someone is writing an essay on digital piracy and that the argument this individual wants to make is that digital piracy is wrong. The main point of an essay is of course expressed in the thesis statement, and what makes the thesis statement so important is that it makes a claim, which the rest of the essay must try to prove. But why, you might ask, is digital piracy wrong? Anticipating a question like that, the thesis statement might look something like this: "Internet file sharing is inherently wrong because it is simply a new form of stealing." The basis for this writer's claim—the data—is the idea that piracy is stealing. We will discuss this example further, but one important thing to notice right now is that a claim comes from data, and that data can easily be an opinion that you will need to qualify or defend later on. Another important observation to make is that the thesis sentence above could be flipped around to read, "File sharing is simply a new form of stealing, so it is wrong."

Claims: You Can't Have an Argument without One

A *claim* is a statement about the data that needs to be proven. For instance, knowing what you do about Internet file sharing may prompt you to claim that it is wrong. Since you know that other people know the same facts but manage to reach different conclusions, your statement launches you into an argument for which you must provide proof. Note that there are several useful tests that can help you determine whether you have made an arguable claim. The first test is whether your statement can be contradicted, and it works in two ways. If information in the data

GRAMMAR **TIP**

Its = belonging to it. *It's* = it is.
"It's obvious that its grammatical approach is superior."

clearly contradicts your claim, then you do not have a claim, or at least not a good one. If you can imagine someone drawing a different conclusion from the same data, or if you anticipate that a reasonable person could demand proof, then you have yourself an *arguable claim*. If your statement meets either criterion, then it has one important characteristic of a claim: it is *falsifiable*, which means that it is essentially false until proven true. Another test is to imagine how you would respond to someone challenging your statement. If your response is to provide facts, then you have not made a strong claim, but a statement of fact. If your response is to provide *reasons*, however, then you are on the right track.

Example A: Billions of dollars worth of digital music and movies were downloaded last year by people who did not pay a cent for them. (statement of fact)

Example B: Internet file sharing is legally and morally wrong because it explicitly breaks international copyright laws while fitting every known definition of theft; moreover, Internet file sharing stifles the production of new music and movies, particularly by less-established artists and companies, and causes significant hardship to many blue-collar workers in the film and music industry. (has a claim)

Can you spot the claim and the data in Example B above? Like in the earlier example, you will notice that the claim (that digital piracy is legally and morally wrong) is connected to some data by the word *because*. You may also notice that there are really two data connected to the claim, and you can probably see right away that the rest of this paper will be about proving that Internet file sharing is legally wrong and that it is morally wrong. In short, the extended thesis in Example B does a good job of presenting the *logical* organization of the paper in such a way that it maps out the *order* and *organization* of the paper too. For that reason, once you've written a thesis statement like this, it will be very difficult to get confused about what should come next, and the same will be true for anyone reading your finished paper.

Did you notice that the second example provides reasons for the claim, but the reasons still need to be explained and defended? That's because while your data is the basis for your claim, you will need to establish why your data is right before your whole argument will withstand cross-examination by a reasonable, well-informed skeptic. And in case you didn't know, the kind of people who mark your papers are professional skeptics.

Warrants: The Validating Principles of Your Thesis

While we will keep Stephen Toulmin's term, our version of the concept of warrant is applied specifically to the task of organizing your essays. In other words, we are adapting his model for analyzing arguments to help you make solid arguments for academic audiences.

The word *warrant* often causes confusion in the classroom because most of you have heard the noun *warrant* before in a different context, mainly on television crime dramas, as a word indicating a legal document needed to arrest someone or search a person's house. Some instructors attempt to dispel that confusion by explaining that warrants are reasons. But when we think of reasons, what we come up with is often fairly subjective, and even arbitrary. As you can see in our discussion of Example B above, what you may consider a good reason for accepting an argument may not, after all, be what your professor considers an adequate reason for believing your argument. *Warrants* are reasons that guarantee that your thesis is true; they are principles. Developing your supports as warrants will put your claim on stronger ground and better fulfill your professor's expectations for your arguments. So, while you may provide the reasons in your thesis statement, your discussion paragraphs should develop those reasons into principles that validate your thesis. The bottom line is, your warrants are the reasons why your audience should believe your claim, and your argument will fail if your warrants are weak.

To illustrate how warrants work, let us keep working with Example B from above. We have already said that the claim that Internet file sharing was "legally and morally wrong" was based on two data: (1) the idea that Internet file sharing violates international copyright law and (2) the similarity between file sharing and theft. But if we think that sentence through, we can see that hidden beneath those data are two principles— two warrants—that support the claim. The first principle is that violating international copyright is legally wrong, and the second

Organizing the Discussion **99**

is that theft is wrong. If you already accept that both statements are true and that they apply to the writer's claim about Internet file sharing, then you are convinced, and you will consider the writer's argument to be true.

Backing: What Makes Your Proofs Solid

However, if you are thinking like a professor, then you will demand evidence to support those warrants. Is violating copyright in fact illegal, and is file sharing covered by any laws? Is theft categorically wrong, and does Internet file sharing really qualify as theft? Answering questions like that is necessary for proving a case, and the way to protect your warrants is to provide backing.

Backing is essentially what you use to substantiate your warrants. It is the one term that troubles some students because backing often resembles what they think of as data, namely, facts, statistics, and quotations. If, however, you think of backing as the facts and examples that "back up" your warrants, and as the hard facts that you can use as solid evidence for your warrants, then the distinction will remain clear. Continuing with our Internet file sharing example, we can see that the writer would need to cite an actual international copyright law and then make a convincing case that the law applied to Internet file sharing. The same would need to be done to prove that downloading a file is really no different from, for example, stealing items from a store. Those facts and examples supporting each warrant are what we mean by backing, and it is only by backing up warrants to your professor's satisfaction that you will be able to prove the argument expressed in your thesis statement.

The relationship between warrants and backing is important, so let us step away from our digital piracy example and look at some others. For instance, consider the claim that there are physiological factors that contribute to conflicts between men and women. In this example, one of the warrants may be that women and men process certain kinds of information differently. To back up that warrant, you would have to cite credible research finding that men and women do, in fact, process certain types of information differently on a neurological level.

In legal settings, lawyers back up their claims with warrants and backing all the time. Imagine that a lawyer is presenting a case (i.e., an argument) like this: "My client is innocent because he was not present when the crime was committed." The plea of innocence is the lawyer's claim, and the reason (the data) is that the defendant was not there. That reason depends on the unstated warrant that the defendant would have had to be present at the crime scene at the precise time of the crime to have committed it. Now, if this reason were all the lawyer had to exonerate her client, they would both be in trouble (the defendant decidedly more so) because the jury would almost certainly require some actual evidence backing up the lawyer's reasoning. So, to satisfy the jury, the lawyer could provide a witness who will provide her client with an alibi, or some other form of proof that her client was, in fact, elsewhere when the crime was committed.

If you are writing about texts, most of your backing will be quotes from the essay, novel, poem or other class material in question. But beware: you must always analyze your quotes to demonstrate with clarity and detail how they support the point you are making. This is also why you should never end a paragraph with a quote. Without your analysis that explains how the quote supports your point and your overall claim, you will have left a gaping hole in your argument. In fact, so many marks are lost through careless use of backing because professors take out their red pens every time they are left thinking, "How on earth did you get this point from that quote?" So, every time you introduce facts, statistics, or quotes to back up a point, always perform these checks:

- Is the backing clear and accurate?

- Is the backing is credible, that is, does it come from a reliable source, and have you cited it properly so that anyone can verify it?

- Is it perfectly clear what point it backs up and how?

- Overall, do the warrant and its backing provide a clear and compelling reason why my thesis is valid?

Qualifiers and Rebuttals

Though they can be the smallest parts of arguments—often no more than a single word or phrase, qualifiers and rebuttals are often absolutely essential to the success of an argument. All too often, the failure to appropriately limit the scope of an argument leaves an otherwise solid claim vulnerable to easy challenge by counter-examples or reasoning.

To illustrate this, let us return to our Internet file sharing example. Some of you have probably objected to the claim because you can think of several instances where the reasoning that file sharing violates copyright simply doesn't hold. For instance, some files do not have copyrights to begin with, others have expired copyrights, and many other files may be legitimately available for free. In other words, there are some situations where that warrant doesn't apply: those instances are called *rebuttals*—weak spots in an argument that need to be closed up. So, in this instance, the writer would need to anticipate that rebuttal with one of his or her own, for instance by limiting the claim to apply only to cases where copyrights were in fact being violated.

While rebuttals protect your argument against instances where a warrant (and thus the claim it supports) isn't valid, *qualifiers* limit the scope or strength of an argument. In this case, saying that "a vast majority of Internet file sharing is illegal" would make the claim much easier to defend, because the writer could, for instance, find some statistics to support the idea that a majority (which is very different from all) of Internet file sharing activity involves music or movies that have internationally valid copyrights.

The mental activity of qualifying your argument and defending it against rebuttals can be compared to the act of building and defending a castle. Qualifying your argument is all about where and how you decide to build that castle in the first place: making a claim that you can't defend is like building a castle in a swamp. In other words, don't make indefensible claims in the first place. For instance, don't claim that you are proving something about all cultures, or all novels, or all of anything if you are examining just one or two books. And if you are aware of some facts or theories that pose problems for your argument, consider narrowing or shifting your focus to give yourself a more viable foundation. To defend your castle against rebuttals, you must realistically acknowledge its most obvious weaknesses and shore them up. You must also anticipate where and how your opposition is mostly likely to attack, so that you can then take appropriate action.

So, qualifiers and rebuttals work with your claims and warrants in different ways. Qualifiers strategically limit your claims, while rebuttals respond to anticipated objections to your claim or the warrants that support it—for instance, by acknowledging exceptions to your warrants. For example, the claim that "downloading music is wrong" clearly needs to be qualified before the author will be able to support it. For one thing, the argument needs to account for the many means of purchasing downloads legally on the Internet, and it also needs to account for the various non-copyrighted musical files that authors and companies have, for various reasons, made available for free download on the Internet. Without appropriate qualification, this argument will be impossible to defend. Qualification is essentially the act of restricting your claim to what you can actually prove: if you think of your claim as a promise to prove your argument, then qualification ensures that you make only promises that you can keep. One simple means of qualifying is to qualify (to give some information that restricts the meaning of) the main noun in your claim. For instance, rewording the claim "Downloading music is wrong" to "Downloading *copyrighted* music *without paying for it* is wrong" will make it significantly easier to defend.

Rebuttals in essay writing usually take one of two forms: cases where warrants do not apply, and known or anticipated objections to claims or warrants. One instance of the former case occurs in Newton's first law of motion: "Every body perseveres in its state of rest, or of uniform motion in a right line, unless it is compelled to change that state by forces impressed thereupon" (Newton 82).[2] Here, the word *unless* introduces the case where the warrant does not apply.

An example of a good rebuttal appears in one known objection to the claim that governments should ban smoking

Organizing the Discussion

GRAMMAR TIP

Your = belonging to *you*. *You're* = *you are*.
"Your monkey is going the same way you're likely to go: into the gutter."

altogether. The rebuttal is that such a policy would impinge upon individual freedom of choice. How do you defend against a rebuttal like that? You could do so by countering that individuals do not have the right to harm others, then making a case comparing the effects of second-hand smoke to other forms of legally culpable negligence. Integrating rebuttals into your arguments will strengthen your arguments dramatically. In fact, defending your claims and warrants against likely rebuttals is not only necessary for strengthening your main argument, but also tremendously effective at clarifying your position, building your credibility by anticipating objections, and illuminating your logic through contrast. So, always remember to try to think of the most likely reasonable objections to your argument, and your essay will be much the better for it.

It's worth noting that anticipating and pre-emptively refuting a strong rebuttal to your argument is often very persuasive because by doing that, you can systematically take down the best reasons why someone might choose to disagree with your argument. And by taking away objections, you leave little room for anyone to disagree with you. So, strong essays always incorporate rebuttals, and when students find themselves slightly short of the desired word count, the C students use "filler," while the A students write a paragraph raising and defeating a good rebuttal.

ORGANIZING YOUR PAPER AROUND YOUR ARGUMENT

Arguments Begin with a Claim

Before we apply the Toulmin model to the composition and organization of discussion sections, let us pause briefly to consider how what we have just learned applies to thesis statements. In the section on thesis statements, you read that each thesis state-ment must make a claim. In the Toulmin model, every argument begins with a claim; this means, conversely, that until you make a claim, you have not said anything that needs to be proven, and your argument can never begin. This simple fact is responsible for the difficulties many first-year students experience in writing essays. Often, they even incorporate what passed as a thesis statement in their high-school English class, but still their pro-fessors scribble comments like "This is not a thesis." The title of this book, *So, Where's Your Thesis?* is in fact a comment I have often thought (but written only once) in response to what some writing instructors call the topical thesis. The so-called topical thesis is great for crafting outlines or for first drafts in which you are exploring the topic and searching for your argument, but it is ultimately not a thesis at all. Here are some examples of topical theses:

1. This essay will discuss the symbolism and significance of the image of the lighthouse in Charles Dickens's *Great Expectations*.

2. In this paper, I will examine the benefits and dangers of recreational marijuana use.

3. This paper will first explore the history of slavery and racism in America, then the second part will analyze how that history forms the background for Toni Morrison's *Beloved*.

All three indicate what the paper will be about, and the third sentence gives the reader some idea of how the paper will be organized (it is thus also a procedural thesis, which we discussed earlier). Not one of those sentences makes a claim, however, and it is the job of a thesis statement to do so. With no claim, there is nothing to prove.

So what is a claim, and how do you know when you've made one? Simply, *claims* are debatable or controversial statements, and you can identify them in a number of different ways. If your friend says something and you express doubt or ask for proof, then your friend has made a claim. If you are reading an article and an author offers facts or reasons to support a proposition, then that proposition is a claim. Claims are statements that have falsifiability: they need proof to be true, and without that proof or justification, claims are simply prejudice—unproven, and possibly unprovable, opinion.

Evaluating Your Claim

The idea of falsifiability also provides you with a tool for evaluating claims—both your own and those of others—in that the strength of a claim is generally proportional to the proof required to persuade your audience. In other words, the success of your essays will hinge not only on whether you make a claim or whether you satisfy its burden of proof, but also upon how strong your claim is to begin with. Lacking ambition, or perhaps fearing being wrong, students will often offer a statement of fact instead of a thesis. For example, consider this thesis statement from an F paper: "The image of the lighthouse occurs many times and in many different contexts in Charles Dickens's novel *Great Expectations*." The statement does make a claim, and the thesis will not be wrong so long as the student can document numerous examples of that image, but the proof required—if a series of examples can be considered proof—is simple and easy to find, so the claim lacks ambition and it is not very interesting.

Your professors will evaluate the strength of your claims, and thereby the potential grade of your essay, not only by the sheer volume of proof implied by your thesis but also by how interesting your claim is. Claims generally become more interesting as the task of proving them becomes more challenging. Though the task of making your claim interesting is limited only by your creativity and insight, there are several tried-and-true ways to increase the strength and interest of a claim:

- contradict a widely accepted opinion

- offer an answer to, or a new understanding of, an established problem or text

- identify a new trend or potential problem

How bold, innovative, or otherwise engaging your claim is will determine to a great extent how interesting your entire essay is, so before you begin writing your discussion, it pays to ensure that your thesis statement provides a worthwhile claim for your discussion to prove.

Many instructors advise students to submit their thesis statements to the "So what?" test, which entails asking, in effect, "Why should anyone care about this argument?" The "So what?" question becomes most valuable, however, when used, paragraph by paragraph, as a strategy for writing your discussion section. In other words, in addition to trying to establish that your thesis is valid, each paragraph should also insist, wherever possible, on why and how your argument matters. By doing so, you will add two characteristics of worthwhile papers that your professors are looking for: *significance* and *relevance*. For example, the interpretive essay on Dickens's motif of the lighthouse in *Great Expectations* would have much more impact if it explained the symbolic significance of the lighthouse to Enlightenment values and explained why characters are so often depicted looking in the opposite direction. Or, an essay on a specific government policy could build relevance by providing examples of how the policy may have tremendously harmful effects upon the very individuals the policy was meant to protect. So, as you work through your discussion, keep in mind that each paragraph must be part of proving your claim—and be vigilant for every opportunity to add significance and relevance to each claim.

BRINGING IT ALL TOGETHER: USING THE TOULMIN MODEL TO ORGANIZE YOUR PAPERS

Once you know that professors are looking for you to begin with a strong claim, then the next step is organizing your discussion section to prove that claim in the most effective way possible. In all the tens of thousands of essays we have read over the years, we have noticed a clear and repeated pattern: in the better papers, every paragraph has a clear topical and logical relationship to the thesis, while in the weaker essays, even if there is a strong enough claim in the thesis statement, the logical and topical relationships between the thesis and each paragraph

> ## GRAMMAR **TIP**
>
> In academic writing, it is considered poor form to begin a sentence with *and*, *but*, *or*, or *so*. If you replace these with *in addition*, *however*, *alternately*, and *therefore*, your essay will sound more formal.

are consistently tenuous or non-existent. Not so coincidentally, those better papers also demonstrate a superior, more sophisticated and better researched grasp of their claim and how it will be received by their professor, while the unsuccessful essays often have whole paragraphs where there is no explicit development or defence of their core argument.

To organize your discussion section using the Toulmin model, you simply begin by recognizing that the function of the introduction is to present your claim as clearly and engagingly as possible, while the function of your discussion is to prove that claim. At the heart of this approach is the requirement that each paragraph (or section in longer essays) provides a reason why your thesis is valid. We will examine three effective techniques for accomplishing that goal: topic sentences, using research, and integration. Of those three, the topic sentence is decidedly the most powerful, so that is where we will begin.

The Topic Sentence Revisited: Its Immense Value as an Organizing Device

We discussed the topic sentence earlier as the key to organizing individual paragraphs. The topic sentence is also critical, however, for calibrating the purpose of each paragraph to the purpose of your entire essay. As we already mentioned and as we will mention again, mastering the topic sentence—the first sentence of each paragraph—will improve your organizational and argumentative abilities, and thus your marks, more than any other type of sentence you will write. The key to the power of topic sentences is that they are, or can be, simultaneously effective at both organizing and arguing. This idea requires some explanation. Organization means not only that all topics are related to each other (your writing instructor may tell you that they form "a coherent topical set"), but also that they are related in some kind of framework, such as an argument or a hierarchy. In other words, organization and argumentation are separate but highly complementary activities because argumentation tends to impart a high degree of logical organization to its topics. Nevertheless, to both organize and argue at the same time, your topic sentences must do the following:

1. Determine the topic of the paragraph.

2. Signal how that topic is related to the central argument of the paper. This may be as simple as repeating a single key word from your thesis statement, but it may sometimes require that you explain, as briefly as possible, how the topic of the paragraph relates to your main argument.

3. Make a point that the remainder of the paragraph will develop and prove. To use our vocabulary from the Toulmin model, that point will ideally be one of your warrants, and the rest of the paragraph will consist of explaining, proving, or qualifying that warrant, providing the necessary backing, and defending it against rebuttals. In other words, your paragraphs will become more effective functional units of your essay when you write with your broader purpose—your thesis—in mind.

USING RESEARCH AS AN ORGANIZING DEVICE

Most upper-year papers, but also the better first- and second-year papers, rely heavily on research to develop their ideas. In fact, the order of the entire essay may often mirror the writer's research journey from one idea, to its rebuttal, to its counter-rebuttal, and so on. Many students learn too late, or never at all, that there is a direct correlation between the quality and quantity of research and the grades they earn. And when students do improve their essays by improving their diligence and proficiency at research, they often credit the infusion of citations and raw data with the improvements in their grades.

THE MECHANICS OF CITATION: MLA, APA, AND CMS STYLES

We've already talked about the MLA and APA citation formats in the section on note taking in Chapter 1. These two formats, and the Chicago Manual of Style (CMS) format, are essentially the same; the order of elements differs due to what the disciplines find important! The important thing to keep in mind with citation is what it is for: in-text reference lends authority to your arguments and shows that you are familiar with texts relevant to your argument, and a "Works Cited" section allows the reader to follow up on particularly interesting sources. So, all forms of citation are designed to show where you got certain ideas or arguments, and to allow an interested reader to locate these sources with a minimum of fuss.

So what is needed in order to locate a source? At a basic level, only the following:

In other words: the writer, the title, the name of the publisher and place of publication, and the date of publication. We will divide the referencing into two parts: in-text citations and works cited section. As we noted in the section on plagiarism in Chapter 1, the in-text citations always need to acknowledge the author, and usually the page number and the date.

BOX **5.2** | ON LOCATING A SOURCE

Who, what, where, when.

STYLE **TIP**

Be aware of common texting shorthand, such as *u* for *you*. These abbreviations have no place in an essay (nor in emails to professors!).

TABLE 5.1

IN-TEXT CITATION

MLA	APA	CMS
In-text information Author, either in a signal phrase or in parentheses. Page number in parentheses.	Direct citation needs author, date, and page number; paraphrases need author and date.	Uses footnotes with whole bibliographic data for first mention and shortened data for subsequent mentions.
e.g., Irwin argues that "monkeys can be dangerous when drunk" (42).	e.g., Irwin (2010) notes, "Monkeys should not be given gin" (p. 43).	e.g., Irwin argues that "monkeys should not be allowed the keys to the liquor cabinet."[1]
OR: Monkeys under the influence of alcohol have been observed to be dangerous (Irwin 42).	OR: According to Irwin (2010), alcohol and monkeys are a dangerous mix.	**Subsequent mentions directly after can use Ibid. with page number;**
Date is not stressed in-text. No use of "p." or "pg."	**Page number only necessary after a direct quote.**	**if not directly after first mention, they can be shortened: Irwin, *Monkeys*, 8.**

Source: Derek Irwin, *Monkeys and Their Vices* (Toronto: Nelson, 2010). Pg. 45.

Works Cited

There are so many different permutations of Works Cited that it would make this book double the size if we tried to list them all. In any case, there are also many excellent sources for finding out how to cite an electronic source, a source with multiple authors, a source without page numbers, and so on.

We have included an appendix to this book outlining the most common types of reference formats you will need, but your best bet is to go for the authoritative guides: *MLA Handbook for Writers of Research Papers*,[3] *Publication Manual of the American Psychological Association*,[4] and *The Chicago Manual of Style*.[5] A fantastic online source that summarizes all of the styles is www.dianahacker.com/resdoc/home.html.[6]

What we will do here is provide you with the information for (1) books and (2) journal articles for each of these three styles.

MLA

1. Last name, First name. *Title of Book*. Publication city: Publisher name, Year of publication. Medium.
   e.g., Martin, Jim. *English Text: System and Structure*. Amsterdam: John Benjamins, 1992. Print.

2. Last Name, First name. "Article Title." *Title of Periodical* Volume.Issue (Year): [page–page]. Medium.
   e.g., Halliday, Michael. "On the Grammar of Pain." *Functions of Language* 5.1 (1998): 1–32. Print.

APA

1. Last name, First initial(s). (Year). *Title of book*. Publication city: Publisher name.
   e.g., Martin, J. (1992). *English text: System and structure*. Amsterdam: John Benjamins. (Note that only the first word of the title and the first word after a colon are capped.)

2. Last name, First initial(s). (Year). Title of article. *Title of Periodical, Volume*(Issue), [page–page].
   e.g., Halliday, M.A.K. (1998). On the grammar of pain. *Functions of Language 5*(1), 1–32.

CMS

1. Last name, First name. *Title of Book*. Publication City: Publisher Name, Year of publication.
   e.g., Martin, Jim. *English Text: System and Structure*. Amsterdam: John Benjamins, 1992.

2. Last Name, First name. "Article Title." *Title of Periodical* Volume, no. Issue (Year): Pages.
   e.g., Halliday, M.A.K. "On the Grammar of Pain." *Functions of Language 5*, no.1 (1998): 1–32.

THE RELEVANCE OF RESEARCHED MATERIAL

As readers and evaluators of all those thousands of student papers, however, we have also noticed that better researched papers are invariably better organized papers. Part of that is simply because any topic you will be required to write on has probably been written about before, and researchable issues are generally part of a debate—an ongoing argument among researchers. As you research your topic, you discover the spectrum of responses and positions, and when you write, you relate your ideas to theirs. A common pattern used by successful students is to introduce another writer's theory or response to the issue, and to then carefully develop how their own ideas relate to it. We should mention that your professors will reward you more when you carefully and respectfully distinguish your ideas from theirs (through the activity called critical thinking) than when you unreservedly agree with them or reject them outright. Ultimately, research is immensely valuable to the organization of your discussion because it can accomplish these three things—and more:

1. Research will put your warrants on firmer ground because it will reveal what rebuttals you should be defending them against. At the same time, while you are writing your first few drafts, always try to develop more warrants than you will need because your ongoing research and writing will reveal which ones actually make your claim stronger and which ones are actually a liability to your argument. Always, always remove those "weak links" from your final draft.

2. It will allow you to find more backing for your warrants: the more credible sources you find to corroborate your ideas, the stronger your reasons will be.

3. It will make the process of writing your essay relatively painless and even quick. If you have thought through your argument fully and researched it thoroughly, then your main point, and even the order in which you should present them, should be relatively clear, and there will be fewer occasions for writer's block.

INTEGRATION

We have found that simply instructing students to ensure that they integrate each paragraph explicitly into their main argument often produces dramatic results. I have found that when I give this instruction to students who connect their paragraphs to their main ideas poorly or not at all, their next essay improves, on average, by one grade point, and sometimes more. Simply possessing the mindset that each paragraph is not just a topic, but part of an overall argument that must be developed and defended, infuses writing with a clearer sense of organization and purpose.

There are two primary means of integrating each paragraph: the first, which we have discussed, is the topic sentence, and the second, which often ends up being one of the least effective sentences in most first-year papers, is the last sentence of each paragraph. As you approach the end of each paragraph, you will have ideally made a point that you have substantiated; once you have done so, however, the last sentence (or two) of your paragraph is your only opportunity to bring that proof full-circle to your thesis. Too often, students assume that their professors will see how their point supports their thesis, but the best papers make the connection explicit, then expand upon it. While it can be effective to create a good, smooth transition from the last sentence of a paragraph to the first sentence of the next paragraph, it is far more important for both sentences to have a clear relation to the thesis statement and to the logic and meaning of your entire paper.

ORDER

Many students agonize over how to order their middle paragraphs, and instructors are often asked what is the correct way

---

GRAMMAR **TIP**

Pronouns ending in *-self* are reflexive, meaning that they are used only for actions that the subject is doing to itself. It is not correct to say, "That monkey attacked Jim and myself." The correct pronoun is *me*, as in "That monkey attacked Jim and me."

The only "self" possible in that situation is the monkey attacking itself!

to order the body paragraphs. There is no one correct way, but there are several approaches and guidelines that you can use. The most important thing to keep in mind is that the purpose of the discussion section is to prove your thesis, and often the thesis statement itself suggests a logical order for your points. Some professors suggest that you lead with your second-best example, and others suggest that you save your best point for the paragraph immediately before your conclusion, but depending upon the nature of your thesis, the next paragraph after your introduction may have to begin with what is sometimes called a "background" paragraph, in which you clarify some of the contexts for your thesis before moving into the main argument. With your knowledge of the Toulmin model, of course, you now know those contexts as data, but you should restrict those bridging paragraphs to one or, at the most, two paragraphs, as it is too easy to become lost in endless contexts and run out of space before your argument can even begin.

SOME FINAL POINTS

The discussion section—the thinking body of your essay—should be the most fun to write. By the time you write it, you will be over the difficulty of finding your topic and developing it into a thesis, and you will have done all our research and outlined your plan of attack. Now it's time to show off what you know. Over the years, we have made it our practice to ask our best students to share the secrets of their success, and in closing, here are some of their tricks for writing discussions:

- Keep a hard copy of your introduction next to you as you write; this will keep you focused as you write each paragraph.

- Don't worry too much about the order at first. Just write each point like a separate mini essay, then arrange them in the best order later, using the topic sentences and closing sentences of each paragraph to fit them in.

- When you write an outline, try to write each point as a full sentence. This is helpful because you can use them as the topic sentences of your paragraphs. In fact, when you've written a good outline with the points and all important quotes right in the outline, the discussion is relatively pain-less to write. It's actually pretty fun to see everything come together so quickly.

- Never take a break in the middle of a paragraph—even if you can't find the right words, try to complete your thought as best as possible, then figure out the exact wording in the revision stage.

NOTES

1. Our version of the Toulmin model is adapted from Toulmin, Stephen Edelston. "The Layout of Arguments." *The Uses of Argument*. Cambridge: Cambridge University Press, 1958. Print.

2. Newton, Sir Isaac. *The Mathematical Principles of Natural Philosophy*. 1st American ed. Trans. Andrew Motte. New York: Daniel Adee, 1846. Print.

3. *MLA Handbook for Writers of Research Papers*. 7th ed. New York: MLA, 2009. Print.

4. *Publication Manual of the American Psychological Association*. 6th ed. Washington: APA, 2009. Print.

5. *The Chicago Manual of Style*. 16th ed. Chicago: University of Chicago Press, 2010. Print.

6. Hacker, Diane, and Barbara Fister, eds. *Research and Documentation Online*, 5th ed. Bedford/St. Martins. n.d. Web. 5 Apr. 2011. <http://bcs.bedfordstmartins.com/resdoc5e/>.

CHAPTER 6

Concluding with Finesse

HAVING THE LAST WORD

The introduction, as we explained in Chapter 2, is where you should strive to make the best first impression you possibly can. Strong introductions engage their audiences by establishing the purpose for the entire paper, stating the thesis, and previewing just enough of the argument to generate some specific focus on the relevance and value of its claims. Your goal in writing the middle section of your essay, the body paragraphs (as we noted in the previous chapter), should be to realize the full potential of your thesis by fleshing out its implications, advancing proofs that validate your claims, and defending your argument against rebuttals. That leads us to a question often asked by students: "If the discussion section has already validated my claim, then what is left to say in the conclusion?" Doesn't the conclusion simply repeat the introduction?

No!

Most students intuitively know that conclusions should relate somehow to their introductions, but few take full advantage of that knowledge by making their conclusions complement their introductions in an effective and meaningful way. In this chapter, we will briefly cover what your professors expect your conclusions to do, then provide several proven yet simple strategies for writing conclusions. Throughout, we will emphasize the value of keeping your purpose firmly in mind, and we will provide some guidelines for writing conclusions that will improve how your professors evaluate your essays. By the end of this chapter, you will have acquired an arsenal of approaches to help you write conclusions that will wow your professors, or at least temper their irritation with the shortcomings of your paper.

First of all, it is important to mention that in some types of writing, conclusions are expected to fulfill some very specific functions and even to follow some specific formulae. For instance, some types of scientific research essays are expected to clarify the study's findings, relate those findings to existing research, account for any differences, and suggest possibilities for further research. In some types of reports, conclusions should focus on recommending policies or courses of action. In humanities essays, however, the highly interpretive nature of the assignments means that conclusions—and the essays they conclude—are often curiously and idiosyncratically tied to the texts and ideas that they are engaging with. Nevertheless, both successful and unsuccessful conclusions to those essays tend to follow a number of recognizable patterns. Let us begin by looking at some of the unsuccessful patterns.

HOW NOT TO CONCLUDE AN ESSAY

The Sudden End

Some essays come to a sudden and unexpected end. Often, those conclusions are no more than two or three sentences long, and have little or no relation to the introduction and the thesis—or to much else in the essay. When asked to explain why they ended their essay so abruptly, students tend to reply in one of three ways:

> It was 3 a.m. and I was tired. I just wrote to the word limit, then stopped.
>
> I thought I had made my point fairly well, and I simply didn't know what else to say.
>
> I didn't want to do anything wrong, and I didn't want to just repeat my thesis, so I just ended my essay. What else could I have done?

The three responses have something in common: they arise from a lack of awareness that the conclusion is not simply the last paragraph of the essay. It is much more than that. The conclusion forms an integral part of every essay's structure, and without a working conclusion, an essay is incomplete. And leaving your essay unfinished will surely cost you marks.

The Repeated Thesis

Generally, conclusions that simply repeat the thesis follow a very recognizable format: "In conclusion" (optional) "this paper has proven" + some iteration of the thesis statement. Using this type of conclusion is slightly better than having no conclusion at all, in that it provides some sense of closure—however artificial. And in cases where the thesis and argument were entirely clear, this type of conclusion sometimes gives professors some belated insight into what the paper was trying to accomplish. In the eyes of most evaluators, this type of conclusion does have some relation to the introduction, but because it simply repeats the introduction, your audience will feel that the conclusion does not complement the introduction, and that the relation between the beginning and the end is mostly empty of significance.

The Surprise Ending

Concluding with a surprise will give your audience a sense of disconnection or incompatibility between the conclusion and the trajectory of the paper to that point. There are several sub-species of this conclusion, however, that are worth mentioning.

One is the conclusion-that-is-really-an-introduction, which typically follows a meandering and unfocused paper, and often ends with a succinct, thesislike statement. Often, that last sentence is far clearer than anything that has come before. In fact, it is sometimes the best sentence of the entire essay. Conclusions like that are dead giveaways that the student is handing in a first draft, and the professor reading such a conclusion may suggest in the margin that the essay be rewritten with the conclusion as the introduction. This type of conclusion fails because it does not meaningfully conclude the essay. If anything, it reminds the professor of the failure of the introduction and discussion preceding the conclusion, and that will not affect the grade favourably.

Two of the other kinds of surprise endings create a disjunction with the rest of the essay, either by raising a new point or by taking off in a new direction entirely. Raising a new point stems from the "save the best until last" philosophy adhered to by some students. You should avoid practicing that philosophy while writing essays for at least two reasons. One is simply that it is difficult to focus on advancing a new point—with all of its specific proofs and illustrations—and on summing up your entire purpose at the same time. Another is that your readers are expecting a conclusion, so they are confused when they encounter a new point. Conclusions that take off in another direction entirely are potentially even more confusing because they can appear to belong to a different essay entirely. In one way, this type of conclusion does precisely the opposite of what effective conclusions do, in that it raises issues that eclipse the essay's focus.

THE KEY ELEMENTS OF SUCCESSFUL CONCLUSIONS

So far, we have looked at several of the ways in which conclusions can fail: they can be functionally nonexistent, they can merely duplicate the beginning, they take off in a new direction, or they can participate too little in the vision that was expressed in the introduction. In explaining why these types of conclusions are problematic, we hinted at the central challenge of writing an effective conclusion: how to *complement* the introduction meaningfully. To be complementary, the introduction and the conclusion must be different, but to make those differences meaningful, the best conclusions pick up where the introduction left off, continuing to expand on the significance of the central purpose of the essay after pausing to prove it first. However, the best conclusions also demonstrate a firm grasp of a key shift that occurs over the course of every essay: introductions present the focus and argument of the paper hypothetically and in abbreviated form; upon reaching the conclusion, however, that focus has been modified and refracted many times by the arguments presented in each paragraph. And without a conclusion that places everything in a broader context and explains what the argument means in its totality, all those little changes could be dismissed as discrepancies, and you will have missed out on the one opportunity you have to consider what you have accomplished and proclaim its merit.

The best conclusions exude a full awareness of the strengths, weaknesses, and full potential of their arguments, and they do that by incorporating three elements that professors expect in a conclusion: they leave no doubt as to where the writer stands on the main issue, they bring the argument to a climactic close, and they give the reader something to keep thinking about after reading the essay.

Take a Final Stand

Conclusions should incorporate a final, brief statement of where the writer stands on the main issue. Sometimes called a "closing argument" or "final judgment," this can be a brief statement of position, and it can be one sentence or less. In its least elegant form, the final stand resembles the "As this paper has proven" + thesis format, but the better written conclusions accomplish the task without saying anything like "as this essay has demonstrated" and without merely echoing the thesis. In order to address the many shifts in focus that occurred over the essay, effective conclusions carefully synthesize the most problematic shifts back into the focus of the paper. The best conclusions repeat key words from the introduction and the argument as they render their final conclusion to the argument; before bringing the argument to a climactic close, you must leave no doubt in your professor's mind regarding whether or how well you have accomplished what you set out to do.

Culmination: The Key to Concluding with a Climax

By the time you've graduated, we hope that you will look back fondly upon the culminations in your best essays. The culmination is the apex of an argument, and the best opportunity for writers to persuade their audiences that their points are unique and profoundly deserving of a response. The best culminations are often the stylistic climax of the paper, where the words breathe with infectious enthusiasm for the argument. Culminations are distinct from the closing argument in that they go beyond answering "What did I argue?" to insist "This is what it means." Your culmination should also do its best to answer the question "So what?" In other words, your culmination is the reply to "How or why does my argument matter?"—and effective culminations provide a compelling reason for accepting their arguments. In terms of evaluation, by taking the value of the thesis and argument to another level, culminations can have a very direct and positive impact on the grade that a paper will receive.

DRIVING YOUR POINT HOME: GIVING YOUR READER SOMETHING TO KEEP THINKING ABOUT

In closing, it is important to note that these key elements of effective conclusions are not necessarily distinct sentences or groups of sentences in the conclusion. They are, rather, very distinct functions that that conclusions fulfill. In other words, the final judgment—your last word on where you stand—may not be crystal clear until the end of the conclusion, but it must eventually emerge without ambiguity. Conclusions can be structured in highly creative and idiosyncratic ways, and just because the best conclusions tend to provide the final judgment within the first few sentences does not necessarily mean that they must. Also, the culmination can take many forms, and it can be combined, to various degrees, with the other elements of the conclusion. But it is the climactic and concluding effects that are critical, not the placement or form of the culmination. Leaving your reader with something to ponder likewise eludes prescription, but there are a number of tried-and-tested strategies for accomplishing this effect. Although we will discuss only three strategies, do not feel confined to just those three: instead, channel your full creative powers into driving home the most important implications of your argument.

The Call to Action

Depending on the type of assignment or the nature of your argument, the best way to keep your reader thinking about your paper may be a call to action. A paper examining the effects of a policy or law, or even a specific state of affairs, may end by proposing a specific amendment to a law or policy, or by proposing new legislation altogether. Or a critical analysis of a particular theory or approach may, on the basis of its conclusion, offer and briefly justify some revisions. The logic underlying the call to action is simple—"my conclusion means that X should do Y"—and it provides an easily grasped, practical application of the argument. The call to action has one drawback, however, that is directly related to its simplicity: it is so intuitive and easily grasped, and often so directly implied by the argument, that your reader may anticipate your conclusion long before you get there. The call to action can therefore seem trite and anti-climactic. So if you use it, ensure that you direct your full creative powers into making your call to action interesting, unique, and compelling. Calls to action are often strengthened by a sense of urgency. For instance, a policy paper may impress the importance of immediate action by stressing the potential consequences of inaction.

Suggest Further Research

Sometimes, essays uncover new problems or issues that have not been resolved, or at least not satisfactorily. In those instances, your response to your conclusion may be to suggest new avenues of research. This ending may appear to be a cop-out if it is executed poorly, but when execute well, it can dramatically improve your professor's estimation of your skills as a researcher, and also of the value of your argument. After all, if your argument has indeed uncovered a matter worthy of a professional researcher's attention and efforts, then yours is no trivial accomplishment. Moreover, if you inspire your professor to pursue that course of research, then your essay can hardly be considered a failure. This type of conclusion can also help you to demonstrate that you know both what your research has accomplished and what your findings mean for other, more senior researchers.

Apply Your Big Idea to a Bigger Context

Maybe you began your paper with big ambitions about addressing very large issues, but then found (or were told by your TA) that you had to dramatically narrow your scope to prove anything. If so, then the conclusion is where you can fulfill those ambitions by suggesting some of the larger implications of your main idea. If you are the type of student who begins with very big ideas and struggles throughout to constrain yourself within a manageable scope, then the conclusion can be your reward for restraining yourself thus far. For instance, your discussion of two or three specific texts or case studies may give you a platform for some inductively grounded speculation about their broader literary or social contexts. Or else your analysis of one poet's use of metaphor may give you grounds for suggesting something about how all poets use metaphor. The logic behind this type of sendoff is to add another level of meaning to your

---

GRAMMAR **TIP**

Don't use apostrophes with possessive pronouns (*theirs, his, hers, its, yours*). These indicate possession all by themselves.

---

argument by drawing out some of its implications for a larger context. Be careful, though: if you fail to establish the connection between your argument and its greater implications, it may seem that you are going off in a new direction altogether.

CONCLUSION TO THE CONCLUSION

Throughout this chapter, we have looked at some of the things that all conclusions should do, and along the way we have suggested a number of approaches that successful conclusions may employ. The strength and value of a conclusion is not, however, measured merely by how it adheres to those guidelines, but by how well it comes full circle and shows the author's full grasp of what he or she has argued and why it is significant. Even after seeing a student struggle through an unclear thesis and then stumble through a discussion, professors will be much more inclined to be lenient if the conclusion can demonstrate that the student understood the problem much better than at first appeared. But ultimately, the biggest significance of a good conclusion is for you: after the long journey of research and the struggle of writing the paper, there can be a tremendous sense of accomplishment in knowing that you're right, together with an incredible sense of confidence in, and enthusiasm for, your ideas. Unleash that enthusiasm into your writing, and you will have ended your essay on a climactic note, and if your introduction and discussion are deserving of that enthusiasm, then you will have just written a really good essay.

CHAPTER 7

The Role of Revision in the Writing Process

In this book, we look at writing as a process, one that more or less consists of three major steps: pre-writing, writing, and revision. In order to justify the necessity for revision, we like to look at the writing process as the "drafting" process. Hence, when we write our essay after having planned it during the pre-writing exercise, what we are really attempting to do during the second step, the writing process, is to get our ideas on paper. In this way, revision becomes not something mechanical but something creative, artistic, and necessary as the last step in the essay writing process. It becomes the means of tying all of our knowledge together, of stepping back and looking at the product and attempting to make it better, stronger, more coherent.

In order for revision to be the tool that we use to create better text, it is important to differentiate between what most writers do—editing—and what we would like all writers to do: revising. For us, editing means making an effort to clean up text. It is what

WRITING **TIP**

Ultimately, revising is more than editing: it's how we approach any text from a different angle—seeing it again. Using grammar and rhetoric as frames, all writers can learn to "see" differently.

we do before we click print on the computer screen. Essentially, editing means fixing grammatical errors, catching typos, and eliminating redundancies and incorrect word choices. When editing, it is often very helpful to read your essay out loud because we tend to hear imperfections before we notice them visually. Another good point to keep in mind is to read with a natural pace.

Remember, if you find yourself pausing unnecessarily or repeating certain sections out loud in an effort to make sense of what you have written, don't ignore that section. Rather, pay attention to what can be done grammatically to improve the sentences or the paragraph. Consider too how you might use punctuation more effectively or whether you have used the right verb tense. Finally, remember that, unlike editing, revision means re-evaluating, re-approaching, and re-examining the essay in an effort to make it accessible, appropriate, and appealing to the audience.

WHAT TO CONSIDER DURING THE REVISION PROCESS

During the revision process it helps to consider how you might begin re-examining and re-evaluating your written piece. We propose that you first ask yourself a number of questions formulated to help you look at your written text objectively:

1. Does the title you have chosen reflect the nature of your essay? Is it intriguing, interesting, and appropriate to the topic?

2. Is the first paragraph (the introduction) appropriate to the thesis? Does the introduction make a good first impression?

3. Do the body paragraphs clearly support your thesis statement, *as you stated it*? Do they offer sufficient and appropriate examples? Do they *explicitly* develop how their ideas support and build upon the thesis in some way?

4. Does your essay offer a satisfying conclusion that offers a final position, a culmination, and a "take-away" thought for the reader to keep contemplating after having read your essay?

5. Have you taken the audience and tone into consideration at all times? Are you writing in an appropriate tense?

Once you have considered your text from this aspect, you should pay some attention to style. Hence, consider what you have written from the perspective of how you have written it. Ask yourself the following questions:

1. In each paragraph, which example is in your opinion the most relevant to supporting the topic sentence? Can you rephrase it in some way? Stylistically, can you adopt any rhetorical devices to help improve the communicative dynamism of the idea you are trying to express?

2. Consider each of the examples in your respective paragraphs. Study your own style. If you tend to write in simple, unadorned sentences, consider taking one of the examples and presenting it differently. For example, if you sentences tend to be simple, why not compose a complex sentence for one of the examples, allowing it to stand out?

3. In each paragraph, underline all cases of the verb *to be*. Consider whether your paragraph would benefit from

Anyways is not a word you can use in an essay. If in doubt, consider this: *any* is like *each*, and in this way, singular in nature. We can say with a great deal of certainty that the following comment makes sense: Any [or each] way you play the game is worth it. But, what of this: Any [or each] ways you play the game is worth it. Grammar aside, remember that some words or phrases are simply part of a dialect (such as *anyways*, for example) and that some words or phrases (such as *anyways*) have meanings that are significant only in an oral context. One friend says to another: "Anyways ... what now?" Where the implication may very well be: Okay, we've talked about everything we can think of; what shall we do next?

Good writers separate writing from speaking. Reserve *anyways* for spoken conversations, if you must. Use *anyway* or a preferable synonym: *nonetheless, hence, thus*.

substituting the verb *to be* with another, more dynamic verb. Dynamic verbs propel your text forward; use them whenever possible.

4. In the text as a whole, examine how often you have used repetition strategically. Remember that strategic repetition is purposeful. It is done for some sort of rhetorical effect, often to remind the reader of an important point or concept. Remove all cases of redundancy, that is, the unnecessary use of repetition.

Finally, as well as considering all of the above, take a moment to read each of your paragraphs carefully. Pay particular attention to how you have constructed your sentences and which words you have chosen.

REVISION AS THE MEANS OF ELIMINATING "CLUTTER"

Wordy phrases or "cluttered" ideas are common problems in undergraduate and college writing. In fact, most of us have at some point seen the comment "wordy construction" next to a paragraph or a phrase of our writing. Fortunately, one aspect of revision is looking at the way we phrase things—of looking at clutter. In this way, just like we might declutter a cupboard or a closet, we can, with some strategic considerations, declutter a phrase, clause, or paragraph. Here are some common "wordy constructions" that tend to make their way into many papers—and their better alternatives.

REAPPROACHING ADVERBS AND ADJECTIVES

Some writers have a flair for the dramatic; they combine adjectives and adverbs in long strings, drawing out the reader's anticipation in an effort to extend the dynamic punch line. Sometimes, this approach is very effective.

It is deceivingly simple upon entering the natural and therefore dirtier and more "primitive" world of the lesser primates to sneeringly discount their abilities, especially upon comparing the habits of these hirsute and scatalogical beasts to the breathtaking achievements of *Homo sapiens sapiens*; nevertheless, close examinations of a number of non-human primates have revealed stunning linguistic abilities, some of them bordering frighteningly close on our own.

For the most part however, simple is better:

> Monkey communication, despite the protests of many linguists, shares a number of properties with what we call "language."

Hence, although adjectives and adverbs do help us create mood, illustrate ideas, and express emotion, in essays, they should be used sparingly and strategically. Keep in mind too that some words are not meant to be modified.

Very unique is an excellent example of the dilemma of modern usage, since something (an entity) cannot be *very* much one of a kind—it simply *is* one of a kind, and hence, unique! In the same stead, something cannot be *more* complete because something that is complete is by necessity whole or finished or even absolute. Further, the following usages are not only awkward but also incorrect: *more perfect* (perfect means without fault, flaw or error, so we cannot grade it), *more unanimous* (unanimous implies the whole or all with nobody disagreeing), *less absolute* (absolute means unlimited, and it implies total power and/or authority; when it is a question of total, we cannot have *less*). In this same vein, we cannot say *less fatal* because fatal implies end. Finally, as a neat close and a good way to end our discussion on modification and revision, consider the very popular and very common phrase *true friend* from the position of logic: someone cannot be a "true" friend unless of course you have "fake ones." In short, keeping on top of how we use modifiers can help to prevent certain types of errors. During the revision process, then, we should be aware of language usage.

Adjectives, Adverbs, and Their Place

Ultimately, revision will not mean eliminating adjectives and adverbs from your writing altogether; it will, however, mean

BOX **7.2**	EXAMPLES OF FAULTY MODIFICATION	
very unique	*less* fatal	*more* complete
more perfect	*true* friend	*more* unanimous
less absolute		

considering how you use those adjectives and adverbs strategically. If you are using more than one adjective in each clause, try examining your choices hierarchically—put those adjectives and adverbs in some sort of hierarchical order; then, remove those that aren't at the top of your list. Leave only those that add vital information to your text. Sometimes, being subtle can be very effective.

As a final point to this section, keep the following in mind: whenever possible, choose specific words instead of a general word (identifying words, like *German shepherd* as opposed to *dog*). To add description and life to your essays, choose concrete words above abstract words. Finally, avoid whenever possible, unless the situation and audience call for it, colloquialisms and slang.

A NOTE ON RHETORICAL DEVICES AND REVISION

We can use language effectively and strategically if we understand what happens when we choose to purposefully manipulate the grammar and the words that we are accustomed to using in an everyday fashion. We make strategic changes to the ways in which we employ language every day in order to accomplish a particular goal: for example, to heighten the reader's awareness of one point as opposed to another in a paragraph where all of the examples are working to fulfil the goals of the topic sentence and to illustrate, define, defend, and/or argue the thesis statement.

Here are some rhetorical devices you may want to keep in mind during the revision process—rhetorical devices that have the power to draw the reader's eye by highlighting one idea over another:

- Asyndeton: the purposeful omission of a conjunction in a place where one would normally be found. Asyndeton can be a very useful device if what you want to accomplish is the feeling of endlessness. "He was a bag of bones, a floppy doll, a broken stick, a maniac" (Jack Kerouac, *On the Road*).[1]

- Polysyndeton: the purposeful inclusion of extra conjunctions in a sentence where only one would normally be used: "Let us eat and drink and be merry!" Polysyndeton can be a very useful device to use if you want to slow readers down, to ensure that they get the entire implication of what you have just written.

- Anaphora: the purposeful repetition of the beginning of a clause in successive clauses. Anaphora is especially useful if you want to jar the reader's attention by purposefully bringing the focus to the beginning of clauses. "We shall go on to the end, we shall fight in France, we shall fight on the seas and oceans, we shall fight with growing confidence and growing strength in the air, we shall defend our Island, whatever the cost may be, we shall fight on the beaches, we shall fight on the landing grounds, we shall fight in the fields and in the streets, we shall fight in the hills; we shall never surrender"* (speech delivered by Winston Churchill in the British House of Commons June 4, 1940).

- Anastrophe: the intentional reversal of the normal order of a sentence for dramatic effect: "Everything else you know."

- Antistrophe: the purposeful repetition of the same word or phrase at the end of successive clauses. "In 1931, ten years ago, Japan invaded Manchukuo—without warning. In

---

*Winston Churchill. Speech: "We shall fight them on the beaches." Delivered to the House of Commons, June 4, 1940.

1935, Italy invaded Ethiopia—without warning. In 1938, Hitler occupied Austria—without warning. In 1939, Hitler invaded Czechoslovakia— without warning. Later in 1939, Hitler invaded Poland—without warning. And now Japan has attacked Malaya and Thailand—and the United States— without warning"* (Franklin D. Roosevelt).

- Climax: the arrangement of words, phrases, or clauses in order of increasing importance, as in "the unalienable rights of life, liberty, and the pursuit of happiness"† (Martin Luther King).

From the position of revision, the goal would be to read each paragraph carefully, looking for instances where you might employ a rhetorical device to help you achieve a particular effect in your writing. Another point to keep in mind is that it is quite easy to change your paragraphs around (using Microsoft Word's Track Changes feature, for example), without having to worry about losing your previous work.

NOTES

1. Kerouac, Jack. *On the Road.* New York: Viking Press, 1957. Print.

---

*Franklin, D. Roosevelt, Address to the Nation. Dec. 9, 1941.
†Martin Luther King, Speech. "I Have a Dream," Lincoln Memorial, Washington, D.C. Delivered August 28, 1963.

CHAPTER
8

Understanding the Grammar of Writing

THE BASIC PROBLEM

If you have ever got an essay back that is a mess of editing marks, this chapter is for you. The basic problem, though, is that in order to understand what the professor has scrawled on the page, you do need to have a bit of an idea of how the English language works. Now, we know that wading through a slew of information on grammar would be painful. And you'd likely ignore it anyway. So we decided that we are going to stick to mainly functional terms to describe what is under the hood of the English language.

So, to begin to understand any sentence, you just need to figure out the following in the realm of *experience:*

WHO Is *DOING WHAT* to *WHOM* Under What *CIRCUMSTANCES?*

We all know that texts are broken down into organizing units, such as chapters and paragraphs, and even though we don't think of it that often, we all recognize the basic units of words and sentences. The essential difference between spoken and written English is that we don't learn to speak in sentences—in fact, sentences are purely artifacts of writing. One definition of a sentence is: "A group of words starting with a capital and ending with a full stop"!

BOX 8.1

The Five Most Common Sentence Errors in Student Writing (and the shorthand professors use to flag it)

1. The Sentence Fragment (SF)
2. Pronoun Reference (PR, P-A)
3. Parallel Construction (II)
4. Subject-Verb Agreement (S-V)
5. The Comma Splice (CS) and Run-on Sentence (ROS)

If sentences are artifacts of writing, and yet we think that we speak in sentences, then how do we actually organize speech? Aside from the observation that not all of us organize our speech—just take a look at most reality TV contestants—we could say that we operate primarily by speaking in *clauses*. A clause answers the above question to a greater or lesser degree: WHO is DOING WHAT to WHOM under what CIRCUMSTANCES?

Of course, we don't speak only in simple clauses, nor do we typically write in them. This chapter will discuss the problems within the simple clause, and then talk about some of the problems with combining them. Next, we will discuss a number of issues that are not really grammatical at all—problems that could be considered "poor form" but not exactly wrong. Finally, we will discuss a way of looking at sentence organization that relates directly to overall text organization. Right off the bat, though, you should simply memorize the list of the five most common sentence-level errors in student writing. By the end of this chapter, you will know exactly how to spot them and how to fix them. Once you can do that, you will be giving your professor a lot less to complain about in your paper, and you'll be losing fewer marks too.

The Simple Sentence = A Single Clause

Our formula (WHO is DOING WHAT to WHOM under WHAT CIRCUMSTANCES) is the limit of what can be handled in a single clause. As a working example, let's take the clause "The monkey kicked Jim in the butt." The monkey is the WHO, and Jim is the WHOM. The monkey is doing some kicking, and it is aiming at a specific location (a CIRCUMSTANCE): Jim's rear end.

Note that the only plural element in our formula is CIRCUMSTANCES—and indeed, it is possible to have several different circumstances in the same clause. We could add that the monkey was kicking Jim "yesterday" (telling us when), that it was kicking "energetically" (how), or "with a frozen boot" (the means). No matter how many of these elements we add, though, we are still left with two participants engaging in an activity (a kicker and a kickee).

Don't take this to mean that you can't have a pluralized WHO or WHOM. It is quite possible for monkeys and apes to work together: "Yesterday, the monkeys and apes energetically kicked the Jim in the butt with frozen boots." In this instance, the linking word *and* gives us more than one participant—but both participants are engaging in the same activity, and so they are both answering the same question. If someone from the SPCA asked us, "Who kicked Jim?" we would answer, "The monkeys and the apes both did." The WHO, the WHOM, and the DOING WHAT are restricted to single instances in the clause. Another DOING WHAT signals a new clause entirely!

The WHO and the WHOM are both participants in the DOING WHAT, and as such they are usually realized by the same form: the *nominal group*.

A Quick Aside: Nominal Groups and Pronoun Reference

The most important thing to remember about the nominal group is that while can be very long, the entire unit can be replaced by a pronoun (the most common pronouns are *I, you, they, we, he,*

BOX 8.2

If you are missing the WHO or the DOING WHAT in your sentence, you will have one type of *sentence fragment*, which is essentially an unfinished *proposition*. For example: "The monkeys living with Jim at the YMCA" or just "Kicked him in the butt."

---

she, and *it*). For example, "The little boy I used to know back in Ottawa kicked my monkey!" "WHO did the kicking?" "He did the kicking!" "The little boy I used to know back in Ottawa" is therefore a single nominal group.

Essentially, three main types of problems that are technically *pronoun reference* issues all come down to confusion over what the pronoun is replacing. Pronouns are an important resource in making writing flow because they provide cohesion to earlier sentences—those WHOs and WHOMs can carry forward to your next point without constant repetition of the nominal groups. In other words, they can make your writing make more sense using fewer words, and that means a better style grade for you.

BOX **8.3** TYPES OF PRONOUN REFERENCE ISSUES

Type 1: Imprecise Pronouns

If the pronoun can apply to more than one nominal group, writers must clarify what it is referring to.

"The boy and his father both kicked *his ball*." Whose ball are we talking about?

More helpful to the reader: "The boy and his father both kicked the boy's ball."

Type 2: Number Issues

In the effort to use gender-neutral language, many writers replace a singular pronoun with a plural.

"A monkey owner must protect *their* pet at all times."

Technically, "*a* person" or "*the* person" ≠ *they*, *them*, or *their*.

Correct: "A monkey owner must protect his or her pet at all times," or "Monkey owners must protect their pets at all times."

Type 3: Vague Reference

Most often a fault of the pronouns *this*, *that*, or *it* at the beginning of a sentence.

"This proves that monkeys should not be kept as pets."

Either replace the pronoun with what you really mean or add in a more specific reference.

Correct: "The prevalence of this abuse proves that monkeys should not be kept as pets."

Back to Simple Sentences: Listing

Part of a well-written paper is the ability to organize points effectively. One means of organizing is through a list. Recall that while we cannot scatter more than one WHO or WHOM throughout the clause, we can have multiple participants in those roles together. However, we need to ensure that these multiple participants are all the same sort, grammatically. Ensuring that these elements match is the heart of *parallel construction*.

Take the assertion "I like X, Y, and Z." Although X, Y, and Z all fulfill the function of WHOM, these participants do not have to be people. It is possible that "I like Jim, Bill, and Mary." However, it is also possible that "I like to eat cheese, apples, and squid" or that "I like to pick daisies, dance with monkeys, and sing all night long." In each of these cases, though, the list items are of the same kind—"Jim," "Bill," and "Mary" are individuals; "cheese," "apples," and "squid" are all items to eat; picking daisies, dancing with monkeys, and singing are all activities.

If I write the sentence "I like to eat cheese, Bill, and dancing with monkeys," the list items are now of different sorts. Do I like to eat Bill?

Parallel construction also works for CIRCUMSTANCES, but for true parallelism they should be of the same type. For example, "We shall dance in the streets, all night long, and without pants" (although informative in its own right) does not have the same rhetorical impact as "We shall dance in our homes, in the streets, and on the steps of City Hall!"

BOX 8.4

Parallel construction also means matching verb forms and number!

e.g., "This paper asserts *that Beowulf is an anti-hero, they* used too much violence compared to today, and *a reader* is interpreting texts differently now" is made up of three assertions in clause form, but the assertions do not "match up."

Compare: "To today's reader, the textual construction of Beowulf is anti-heroic, due to cultural shifts in *the concept of the hero, the text*, and *the role* of violence in problem solving."

BOX **8.5**

Because the pronouns are singular, these same pronouns must be matched with both genders. We cannot write, "*Everyone* brought *their* bottle to the party"—we must instead use "*Everyone* brought *his or her* bottle to the party" (though we could say "All the people brought their bottles"!) Essentially, we want to make clear that everyone is a singular pronoun and that in this context, it embraces both genders equally as singular pronouns. Using "their," as such, is grammatically incorrect.

The Simple Sentence: Subject–Verb Agreement

The only times that subject–verb agreement is really a problem to those who speak English as a first language are those occasions in which the WHO is so complicated that the DOING WHAT refers to the wrong words.

For example, the first time I wrote the above sentence, I used *is* instead of *are*. The confusion stemmed from the massive WHO in the above sentence: "The only times that subject–verb agreement is really a problem to those who speak English as a first language ..." Had I chosen to say, "The only time" I would of course have used *is*.

The problem goes back to the nature of the nominal group. Technically, a subject such as "a bag of tacks" refers to the "bag," and not the "tacks," and so we would write "A bag of tacks is expensive" and not "are expensive."

Another point of confusion is with certain pronouns. *Someone, everyone, anyone,* and *no one* are all singular because they are all versions of the word *one*, which is singular. So we should write, "No one among the students *is* expected to pass," and not, "No one among the students *are* expected to pass."

COMBINING CLAUSES: COORDINATION AND SUBORDINATION

If you cannot effectively combine clauses, your writing will quite simply sound choppy and somewhat ridiculous. However, if you

BOX **8.6**

I love my monkey + my monkey loves me (coordination *and*).

I love my monkey > my monkey loves me (subordination *because*).

> I love my monkey, my monkey loves me (subordination *if*).

do not combine effectively, your writing will have no logical structure. Coordination is the strategy of combining items along the same level—think of it as a giant equals sign. Subordination is the choice of making one clause dependent on another—think of it as a greater than or less than sign.

Coordination

The final grammatical problem that we will treat is the issue of comma splices and run-on sentences. The reason that we can treat them together is simple: they are the same problem, but one has a comma and one does not.

Essentially, when we put together clauses, there are a few different options. The first is simply to leave them as separate sentences:

"I like my monkey. He is very cute. We sometimes fight."

We read these three sentences as related because of their use of pronouns: the WHOM of the first sentence becomes the WHO of the second, and the two WHOs in the first two sentences become the WHO of the final one. It would be quite strange to assert that these three sentences could be taken to mean "I like my monkey. My friend is very cute. My sisters and I sometimes fight."

It would be even stranger to assert that the "I" in the first, the "my" in the second, and the "my" and "I" in the third were different people! So, even though the first three sentences are cohesive thanks to pronoun use, a criticism of texts filled with simple sentences is that they read as "choppy." Fluid writing relies on a number of features, aside from just using pronouns properly. For example, we could add in so-called transition words to create a logical flow.

"I like my monkey. Moreover, he is very cute. Nevertheless, we sometimes fight."

BOX **8.7** FANBOYS

For

And

Nor

But

Or

Yet

So

The addition of these transition terms does not alter the basic fact that there are still three simple sentences, but it does link each of these sentences beyond its initial capital and final stop. However, it is possible to link them directly in two different ways. The first way is to treat each clause as an equal, a process known as *coordination*. Coordination creates a logical relationship of equivalency. In order to coordinate, we use either a coordinating conjunction or a semicolon. The traditional way to remember the seven different coordinating conjunctions is through the mnemonic FANBOYS.

"I like my monkey, for he is very cute, but we sometimes fight."

The semicolon allows us to connect independent clauses without the bother of a coordinating conjunction, and also allows us to use transitional words inside the sentence:

"I like my monkey, for he is very cute; however, we sometimes fight."

Strategically, you can consider the *semicolon* as a device that allows you to show the reader that there exists an intricate connection between the two ideas; that essentially, by separating them into two clauses and punctuating them with a period something would be lost. Semicolons are powerful punctuation markers—they are like periods, but they also show connections. Good writers use semicolons strategically for rhetorical effect and for the message that they send to the reader. Note, however, that, as with all good things, overusing the semi-colon actually

BOX **8.8**

A subordinate clause on its own is a sentence fragment:

"If only that waiter hadn't touched the monkey."

Solution: add an independent clause:

"If only that waiter hadn't touched the monkey, this soup would have tasted much better."

weakens its power as a punctuation marker. So use it wisely by saving it for your best points.

Note: Coordination creates *compound sentences.*

Subordination

The other sort of clause combination creates *an unequal relationship between clauses*, and it is called *subordination.* Subordination also creates a type of logical relationship, but in this case it is a dependency relationship, not an equivalency relationship. There are several different types of subordination, but the most common uses subordinating conjunctions. Subordinating conjunctions are words such as *because*, *if*, and *when.* Employing them in a clause makes it dependent on another clause around it:

"I love my monkey because he is very cute, even if we sometimes fight."

Note: Subordination creates *complex sentences.*

Good writing combines sentence types; you can use simple, compound, and complex sentences to vary sentence length and internal logical relationships. You can also create compound-complex sentences; however, there is a limit to the amount that a reader is willing to logically follow. Simple is sometimes best!

When you use subordination, it is often helpful to begin with a dependent clause in order to flow from the prior sentence, or to demonstrate knowledge of a set of circumstances ("Because my monkey steals my gin, we often fight.") Check out Chapter 4 for helpful hints on logical relations.

BOX **8.9**

A *run-on sentence* ignores the need to coordinate or subordinate clauses:

"I love my monkey he is very cute we sometimes fight."

A *comma splice* tries to separate independent clauses with a comma:

"I love my monkey, he is very cute, we sometimes fight."

To fix:

- Split into separate sentences

  "I love my monkey. He is very cute. We sometimes fight."

- Coordinate

  "I love my monkey and he is very cute, but we sometimes fight."

- Subordinate

  "Because I love my monkey only when he is very cute, we sometimes fight."

- Mix it up

  "I love my monkey because he is very cute, yet we sometimes fight."

GRAMMATICALLY CORRECT BUT POOR FORM

As we saw with the advice to vary your sentence types, you will find that some readers will take issue with your writing style even if your grammar is correct—or at least follows the principles of traditional grammar considered acceptable in much of today's writing. However, the prudent writer will know his or her audience, and write accordingly. If you write in an academic setting, you will be held to a very high standard of writing, and these tips will help you to transcend mere grammatical correctness and take your style to the next level of execution.

Repetition and Redundancy

It is a poor choice to employ the same words or phrases over and over again. Repetition, especially of a main word or concept, is sometimes unavoidable, but such strategies as the employment of pronouns and synonyms can greatly reduce your dependency on the same word or term. However, you usually do not want to employ the same sentence-level concepts or arguments by rephrasing. Such reiteration is distracting, and it dilutes your arguments. There have been occasions where I have been able to relieve an essay of over half of its words, simply because the writer is telling me the same thing again and again. Just because that writer reaches the word count does not mean he or she will do well!

Wordiness

Wordiness can be related to redundancy, but they are not exactly the same thing. We can use an awful lot of words to say a very simple thing! However, very often, the less you write, the clearer your point is (and the more lucid your style appears). For example, instead of writing "due to the fact that," simply write "because." Instead of "being under the impression that," "believing." Remember, although you are likely writing to a page count, professors prefer a paper with excellent prose and clear points that comes in under the recommended word count to a paper that is convoluted and difficult to decipher but that happens to clock in at the word count; quality always trumps quantity!

Clichés

Quite simply, clichés weaken your writing. Such expressions as "look before you leap," "sick as a dog," or "bite the bullet" at one time may have held original meaning, but that meaning has

---

STYLE TIP

Great turns of phrase should not be employed in large numbers or in rapid succession. Instead, intersperse the work with them—your readers will savour them so much more!

---

long faded. Good prose involves playing with words in such a way that their original use grabs the reader's attention and engages his or her imagination.

Clichés have the opposite effect: they convey a watered-down version of the experiential content of the expression. Pretend that you are going cheese shopping for a great cheese lover. Do you grab the cheese spread just because it's the first cheeselike product that you come across? If you do, will the cheese connoisseur appreciate the obvious lack of effort on your part? Or do you head to the deli section to peruse the finest in cheesy comestibles that the store has to offer, tailoring your purchase to the type of occasion (wine, company, crackers) that is the best fit? Even one well-turned phrase can convince the reader that you are a brilliant writer.

Tense Shifts

Shifting verb tense between past and present is a real grammatical problem if it occurs within a sentence, but it is also a problem when, as often happens, it occurs from one sentence to the next. Part of the problem is the convention that we must write about texts in the present tense:

> In *The Problem with Monkeys*, Zippy argues that "Most monkeys do not enjoy being kicked" (11).

This convention is standard, despite the simple reality that these texts were written in the past and our having read them is (we hope!) also in the past. However, research that is complete is referred to using the past tense:

> In his study on monkey-on-monkey violence, Zippy found that kicking was quite rare.

The real problem arises when a writer is inconsistent in his or her approach.

First Person

Many secondary school teachers simply tell students that they are not allowed to use *I* or *me* in an essay, for very good reason.

Inexperienced writers tend not to use the first person voice effectively. Phrases such as *I think* or *I believe* do not add anything to an argument; in fact, they detract from it by being absolutely redundant, or by presenting your observation as subjective when you could have claimed some objective value for it. Everything in an essay that is not cited from elsewhere has an implied "I think" in front of it. We suggest that you avoid the first person singular, and also such cheats as the pronoun *one*. *One* tends to simply replace *I*, and when it does, it sounds stilted and subjective. Also avoid the use of the "royal" *we*, since it implies one of two things, both of them problematic: (1) that your reader is within that group (who may not appreciate the presumptuousness of it) or (2) that you are excluding your reader (who may then have an adversarial reaction).

Second Person

Much like the problem with using *we*, using *you* in a text also either constructs or alienates the reader. When a writer has a very firm knowledge of a projected reader (such as in this book, where we presume you are reading to find information about writing essays), it may be excusable. However, in more formal writing, where the reader is generally your professor, the use of "you" becomes more disconcerting, especially because "you" assumes that the reader and writer share the same viewpoints: a solidarity of sorts, which should not be breached. There is no way to account for readers and writers to share the same points of view, so it is best to avoid the dilemma and stick to the third person.

Numbering

How to treat numbers in essays is largely dependent on the discipline and instructor, but there are a few observations that generally hold true. For example, do not begin a sentence with numerals. If it seems awkward to spell the number out, then rewrite the sentence such that the numerals appear after a CIRCUMSTANCE. Also, numbers from nine and under are usually going to be spelled out, unless they are part of decimals, percentages, fractions, scores, statistics, times, days, years, or large round numbers. Any numbers 100 and over are typically not spelled out. However, different people have different approaches to the numbers between 10 and 100—some guides suggest that any numbers of fewer than three words be spelled out ("ninety-seven monkeys" versus "101 monkeys"), while others suggest that anything over 10 uses numerals. We suggest that you choose a method and stick to it consistently throughout your text.

Passive Voice

The passive voice is where we take the WHOM and move it into the WHO position. So, instead of writing the active "Jim-Bob kicked my monkey," we can write the passive "My monkey was kicked (by Jim-Bob)." The beauty of the passive voice is that we don't need to include the doer at all—Jim-Bob can be completely removed from the equation. However, this benefit is also the weakness of the passive voice. When we don't know whodunit, it leaves us feeling unfulfilled. So, instead of protecting the identity of Jim-Bob, out him. Tell the world he is a monkey-kicker. A good exercise is to go back through your writing and highlight the number of times you use variations of the verb *to be* (*am, is, are, was, were, been, being, be*), then ask yourself: Do I have other choices here? Am I hiding who is doing what to whom? And if so, why am I doing so? Note: Sometimes the passive voice is absolutely the right choice: for pointers, look at the final section of this chapter, on text organization.

Poor Modification (a.k.a. Is my participle dangling?)

Technically, modification is a grammatical issue, but it leans toward being more of a problem in interpretation. Problems with modification generally result from modifying by afterthought. Part of the problem is that modification can be either a CIRCUMSTANCE or part of the WHO or WHOM. If a reader can't tell whether you are modifying one or the other, there is a failure in communication. "I hit the man with the tire iron" could be seen as either horrible abuse (the man was hit with the tire iron) or legitimate self-defence (I had to hit him;

he had a tire iron!). Another issue with modification is when the CIRCUMSTANCE does not match the WHO or WHOM of the clause—depending on whether it is sentence-initial or -final (comes at the beginning of the sentence or at the end). "Protecting our nation's citizens, new legislation was passed to restrict striking men with small beards." Here, the people protecting the citizens are the legislators, not the legislation (which is hidden because of the passive clause). Rewrite to include the WHO: "Protecting our nation's citizens, law-makers passed legislation to restrict the hitting of people with small beards."

Capitalization

Some capitalization, such as the capital at the beginning of a sentence, could be considered grammatical in nature. Other capitalization, such as those for proper nouns, has to do with word conventions. Spell-checkers catch errors in some of these conventions, but you can't rely on them to catch words that can be both proper nouns and just regular nouns—Turkey the country versus turkey the delicious Thanksgiving treat, for example. Most writers know that we capitalize names (Jim-Bob), days of the week (Wednesday), months (May), holidays (Labour Day), nationalities (Uzbekistani), languages (Swahili), religions (Taoist), and historical events or periods (the Renaissance). When we are talking about a specific place or region, we also capitalize (the North), but we don't capitalize direction ("Go north, young man!") There are also some so-called proper adjectives, which use proper nouns as their base. *Shakespearean*, *Torontonian*, and *Martian* are just some examples, but note that even though *the Bible* is capitalized, *biblical* is not. Finally, titles of various sorts are capitalized (*Apes, Language, and the Human Mind* is a book title, while Prime Minister of Monkeyland is a personal title). Note, however, that articles and other connecting words are not capitalized (such as *a, an, the, in, of,* or *to*) unless they begin a section title or subtitle. Fortunately, style guides exist to clarify the rules surrounding capitalization and essay writing. Consulting the style guide your professor recommends (either APA or MLA) will help you determine further how to deal with capitalization

THE CLAUSE AS MESSAGE

It is also possible to think about the organization of your clauses as being a part of the overall organization of your essay. This approach relies on the information structure of the English language: namely, that we start a message with information we consider "Given," and move on to what we consider "New."

Theme

Experiential elements at the beginning of a clause (WHO, DOES WHAT, WHOM, and CIRCUMSTANCES) are part of the *Theme*.[1] We organize our clauses by using the Theme as a kind of agreed-upon bit of information, thus making it quite an important concept in essay writing. In simplest terms, the Theme of the clause is what comes first. The first position is the most important position because strategic information often makes its way into the Theme or the first position of a clause.

In the previous section, we mentioned the use of the passive and suggested that it tends to be used too often in student writing (which is generally true!). The passive does, however, have an important role in the Theme—it allows us to "front," or bring to attention in what might be considered a "marked" way, what is generally acted upon, such as our objects of study. We said a moment ago that the Theme, what comes first, is often Given information. Hence, when a clause begins in the passive voice, the writer is ultimately putting into first position—the Theme— something that normally would not have been there had the clause been written in active voice. In this way, then, that clause, that sentence, and that choice becomes fronted and marked.

Take the following:

"Many children enjoy outdoor activities such as fishing."

versus:

"Outdoor activities such as fishing are enjoyed by many children."

Both of these clauses are experientially the same: "many children" (WHO) are enjoying (DOING WHAT), and it is "outdoor activities such as fishing" (WHOM) that they enjoy. What is different is the focus of the message: in the first, we are more likely writing about the children, and in the second we care more about the outdoor activities.

In a single clause, this distinction is meaningful but not particularly crucial. However, across stretches of text, we can look at the patterns of Theme to determine whether the writer is sticking to his or her message or instead including information that is not relevant.

The Topic as Hyper-Theme

If you trace the Themes of clauses in a given paragraph, you will notice that they generally cluster around a topic—that is, if you have a coherent essay! The topic is called the *Hyper-theme*. The Themes are consistent because you and the reader have agreed on what you are negotiating, and the rest of the clauses are designed to provide the particular points a writer wishes to assert. So, although you don't want to be repetitive in your writing, you *will* want to ensure that each paragraph has a clear Hyper-theme, which allows the reader to clearly follow the topic under question.

The Thesis Statement as Macro-Theme

You'll also notice that the thesis statement is often structured in such a way that it introduces the argument and then lists the supporting proofs. In this way, the information in the "New" part of that particular clause becomes the overall Theme, or *Macro-theme*, of the subsequent paragraphs. Let's examine the following thesis:

> "Beowulf can be considered a good lord of his time because he committed great feats of arms, gave proper respect to his overlords, and distributed many valuable gifts."

It is clear that the central point is that the writer considers Beowulf to be a good lord (which is a full clause representing the central argument) and that the following paragraphs will discuss how his feats of arms, respecting his betters, and gift-giving support this assertion. Thus, these points from the Macro-theme will be picked up as subsequent Hyper-themes, and those Hyper-themes will work as the Themes of individual sentences throughout the text.

Viewing a text as a selection of Themes, Hyper-themes, and Macro-themes also illustrates why a proper outline is so important to your work—outlines ensure that you have an overall consistency of themes, which in turn ensures that your reader is clear on what is being proposed and argued. An incoherent essay will certainly not make for a good read!

NOTE

1. Note that a full discussion of Theme, Hyper-theme, and Macro-theme can be found in Martin, J.R. *English Text: System and Structure*. Amsterdam: John Benjamins, 1992. Print.

CHAPTER

9

Tying It All Together

Writing is never easy. Writing is a messy business—something that takes time and practice. A *lot* of practice. Throughout the pages of this book we have endeavoured to provide you, the reader (and writer), with some helpful tips to make the process of writing simpler. But practice is what shall ultimately prevail.

Often, as instructors, we discuss the pitfalls of the writing process, and we never fail to point out that the major one is giving up too soon. In fact, much has been written on the art of simply writing as a means of developing style and sustenance. A number of helpful tools exist: Free writing, or the writing before the writing exercise, often helps many students move from writer's block to effective communication. One particularly helpful systematic strategy is what we like to call the "imitation journal." When you find a piece of writing that you find effective or provocative, try to emulate it in some way. You can try changing the subject matter of the piece, or the intended audience, or the basic organization; more on this in a moment. This exercise works because it is based on the cornerstone of good writing: critical reading.

Suffice it to say that good writers are avid readers. We don't know what we like until we have seen it in practice, and we can't really know what it looks like until we practise producing something similar ourselves. Over the years, in our classes at various universities, we have made the simple suggestion to students that one of the most productive ways of improving their writing is through the act of writing and reading itself. So, as our close to a book dedicated to the writing of essays, let us present you with this methodology.

THE IMITATION JOURNAL EXPLAINED

1. Find a writer whom you genuinely admire and consider why you admire this writer. Ask yourself: Is it because of the subject matter or is it because of the way in which the writer writes about the subject matter? The answer to this question is paramount. For example, if you like vampire novels, can you say you like all vampire novels equally? Probably not. In actuality, what you probably like is the subject matter (the vampire genre) and the way in which the writer you admire presents the turn of events in the novel itself. Find a writer who writes about what you like to read and then spend some time looking at how that writer writes.

2. Once you have found your writer, look at the words that writer uses. Examine the sentence structures. Focus on the rhetorical devices. If you are spurred on to read quickly, is it because the subject matter is so enthralling, or is it because the subject matter coupled with the style of the text is appealing?

3. Mimic the style of your writer. Each week for about 15 minutes, spend some time looking closely at the sentences that you have found so appealing. Using a computer or (even better!) a pad of paper and a pen, transcribe word for word one paragraph of the text you admire. Then, attempt to mimic the style of that paragraph, paying particular attention to punctuation, verb choice, sentence style, voice, and mood. Choose a topic that is different from the topic of the paragraph you are imitating; copy just the sentence structure. You will discover that it is more than topic that appeals to you as a reader—it is also style.

4. Change your writer once a month, and see what happens if you change the genre of text as well. Each week choose a different paragraph from the text you are focusing on. By switching writers, you are embracing different writing styles, and by changing text types, you will develop a mastery in various approaches to organizing messages. Further, by changing writers and imitating them, you are developing your own style. Most important, having your own style is the key to ownership of your writing, and you will almost certainly be proud of the work you have done in your own voice!

Good writing requires us to pay attention to many things: audience, tone, style, grammar, cohesion, and coherence. It requires that we practise the art of writing and that we read to increase our knowledge of the variations available. We have stressed in the body of this book that essay writing is a process of pre-writing, writing, and revision. We hope that you will view this process as one that can be productive to you.

Good luck in your writing!

HOW ESSAYS ARE MARKED

THE LOW-DOWN ON GRADING

We professors were once students too, and one of the main impulses for writing this book was the frustration and anxiety we experienced trying to answer the question "What does my professor want?" We believe firmly that people have a much better chance of succeeding when they understand how they are being evaluated, and that's why we have always made a practice of giving a copy of our essay marking scheme to our students.

Please understand that what you will read in this appendix is just one example of how essays are marked. Many professors will use slightly different marking schemes, with varying emphasis and different weighting of certain elements. In fact, we ourselves will use one marking scheme in a literature class (where analysis and argument are very important) and another in a writing class (where organization, style, and mechanics have a heavier weighting). Nevertheless, we do use marking schemes because they help ensure that every student is evaluated on the same scale. And that, in our books, is the definition of *fair*. What follows is an example of a marking scheme we use in an undergraduate class where writing is very important. Even within this category of essay writing, the weightings might change from professor to professor. Also, your professor could choose not to grade you explicitly on style and instead re-allocate those marks elsewhere.

What the Marking Categories Mean
Organization

Organization includes the presentation and structuring of ideas at the paragraph level and the essay level, especially in the introduction and conclusion.

- **Introduction:** should distil the overall aim of the paper into a thesis statement, complete with a proposed **method of proof** that **outlines** or suggests how you will prove your **argument.**

FIGURE A-1

Essay Marking Scheme

ORGANIZATION	10
STYLE	5
SENTENCE AND PARAGRAPH MECHANICS	10
ARGUMENT	15
ANALYSIS	15
COMPREHENSION OF MATERIAL	15
ILLUSTRATION AND PROOF	15
CITATION (DOCUMENTATION)	5
ANSWERS THE QUESTION	10
TOTAL	**100%**

- **Conclusion:** should assess accurately the merits and weaknesses of your argument, drawing appropriate conclusions that result logically from your analysis. The conclusion should end with a compelling sense of why your arguments should be accepted or why they are significant. Do not merely repeat your thesis.

- **Paragraphing:** should break up the essay into logically and topically distinct functional units, signal divisions, control pace, and facilitate logical development. All paragraphs should illustrate, develop, or substantiate the thesis (creating relevance and coherence) and link fluidly with other paragraphs (building cohesion) to form the body of the essay. Furthermore, they should be structured clearly, consisting of a **topic statement** that communicates the topical and argumentative focus of the paragraph; a body consisting of examples, analysis, and illustrations that support the topic sentence; and a conclusion that clearly and productively integrates the paragraph into your overall argument.

- **Development:** should organize the points and examples strategically to optimize the effectiveness of each paragraph, point, and example in fulfilling the overall purpose. The choices you make at the outlining stage will significantly impact the overall shape of your paper, so choose your development strategies wisely as you plan your paper.

Style

The style grade considers the writer's mastery of the English language in communicating ideas, advancing arguments, and creating a sense of coherence. Style encompasses both sentence-level concerns—such as tone, diction, and lucidity—and effective use of rhetorical forms, such as parallelism. Effective stylists use words and sentence structure to forge and animate relationships between ideas. Lucidity is imperative, and it can be accomplished only through clarity and brevity. Stylistically superior papers bare their ideas and evidence, and do not obscure them behind a veil of adjectives or wordiness. Diction is the writer's palate, and effective stylists choose their words in ways that communicate their ideas both clearly and powerfully.

Sentence and Paragraph Mechanics

Mechanics include grammar, sentence structure, wording, phrasing, spelling, and punctuation, all of which should be flawless in an adequately edited and revised academic paper. Mechanical errors detract from the clarity and effectiveness of your argument and seriously compromise your credibility as its advocate.

Argument

This category looks at the strength and sophistication of the argument. The thesis statement is a very important component of the mark for this category, so it should present a clear, ambitious, and arguable claim. The supporting argument should be specific and detailed, logically developed, and sufficiently illustrated. Ask yourself: Does my argument elicit belief? And does my paper develop its argument through critical and logical analysis of textual material (strong), or through generalizations and summary (weak)? Does my argument explicitly prove what my thesis claimed, and did I meet the specific requirements of the assignment (both important for a strong paper)? Does the scope of my thesis correspond to the scope of the actual argument and proof? Does the scope avoid being too broad or too narrow, and is it gauged appropriately to the conditions of the assignment, such as the word limit and the required number of secondary sources? Does the argument remain focused and coherent throughout? Are the body paragraphs used to effectively develop the argument throughout?

Analysis

In analytical papers, the mark for analysis is sometimes worth more than 50 percent. This category evaluates the student's use of logic and course concepts to analyze the issue. Perceptiveness, creativity, and the ability to break down complex problems elegantly and accurately are key to receiving a high mark in this category.

Comprehension of Material

Many professors use essays to evaluate how well a student understands certain texts or concepts, and this category is very important in such papers. Almost all essay questions on final exams are comprehension-oriented. To do well in this category, you must demonstrate that you know the concepts that appeared in class or in texts. Research papers have a strong "comprehension" component, to the point that this category is often called "research." This category is very simple: if you know your stuff, you get the marks.

Illustration and Proof

Aristotle once said, "He who asserts must prove," and he was right: an argument is only as credible as the quality and quantity of evidence presented to support it. Writing an essay is very much like being a lawyer, because you need to prove your case—and without properly presented and validated evidence, you will fail to persuade the jury (in this case, your professor or TA). Otherwise stated, reasonable doubt = you lose. A successful argumentative essay never leaves the credibility of its argument open to easy challenge from logical or textual evidence. Each paragraph should explicitly and tangibly contribute toward proving your overall case. Always remember that no conclusions can be drawn independently of evidence. Every point must be validated by an authority other than yourself (such as a primary text, a scholarly authority, or logic). That source, in turn, must be made credible and relevant through your own analysis and illustration. You should begin with the view that your audience is neither compelled nor remotely inclined to believe anything you say, and that you must therefore establish your own credibility by supporting everything that you assert, anticipating rebuttals and defending your views against them through careful analysis.

Citation (Documentation)

Adequate and correct documentation not only directs your readers to your sources (establishing validity), but also imparts a professional appearance to your paper; assiduous and flawless documentation project a writer who is honest, carefully researched, and therefore credible. Make sure you use the correct style (i.e., MLA, APA, or Chicago).

Answers the Question

Even well-written papers can be failed outright if they are on the wrong topic or reading or do not answer the question or meet the assignment's requirements. When you are given very specific instructions, always make it very clear in your introduction how your paper responds to the instructions you were given. Note: For instructors, papers that do not answer the question are prime suspects for plagiarism.

How Professors Use Those Categories to Mark Your Papers

As you can see, the categories all have a weighting, and in most instances, it's simply a matter of assigning a grade for each section (e.g., 6 out of 10) and adding up the marks to yield a mark out of 100 percent, which is then expressed as a percentage or a letter grade. Many experienced professors jump straight to the letter grade because they have marked thousands of papers and know all the math in their heads. Also, they probably have another hundred papers sitting on their desks, and it's much easier simply to write a letter grade on a paper, jot down some comments, and move on to the next paper.

Although guidelines may differ from institution to institution, here is the rough translation of number grades to letter grades:

90–100	A+
85–89	A
80–84	A–
77–79	B+
73–76	B
70–72	B–
67–69	C+
63–66	C
60–62	C–
57–59	D+
53–56	D
50–52	D–
0–49	F

Pay special attention to two things: the plain letter grades (e.g., A, B, C) have a larger range, and while the A+ is large, it begins 10 marks higher than the A– range. By comparison, it is only 7 marks from B– to B+. That is a small indication of how difficult an A+ is to attain, and it's one reason why you should be very proud of yourself whenever you do receive an A+. It's also worth noting that some schools use different scales, such as not having minus grades. One school we know of even has a grade "E" to indicate a "marginal fail"; in that school, a grade between 45 and 49 percent earns you an E, which means that you failed, but you can try the course again if you want a shot at earning a better grade. Even if you go to a school like that, however, the official grading system will probably resemble the one above, and it is in your interest to know it and understand it. There is an important life lesson here: understanding expectations is the key to meeting them.

You may be wondering, "If you start with numbers, why don't you just give a percentage grade and be done with it?" That is a good question. About 90 percent of the time, the final letter grade you get will in fact be a direct translation of the percentage grade that you earned. But in writing-focused courses, your teachers understand that you may stress out on the final exam and not finish all the questions, or get off to a very bad start in the course but improve dramatically in the second half of the course, only to fall a fraction of a percent short of a B or C. For those cases, because professors like us want your final grade to be an accurate reflection of your *final standing* in the course, we treat your final letter grade as more important than the absolute numbers. So, if your second-half standing was consistently high, we might go back and re-enter a 75 as a 76 to give you that quarter of a percent that you were short. But only within the letter grade that you earned, and only if you really deserve it.

Although marking schemes are time-consuming to use, they are invaluable to less experienced teachers, and we know from experience that they are very, very helpful to students. After all, if you can see that your argumentative skills and grammar are costing you a total of 15 percent on every essay, then you will be more likely to focus on improving your skills in those areas.

In closing, there are some points we would like to clarify about the grades in each category. Many students ask us, "Where did I lose all those marks?" when the problem is very often that *they never earned the marks in the first place.* In the case of argument, for instance (which can be worth over 50 percent in a philosophy paper), an argument doesn't have to be obviously wrong or illogical for you to "lose marks"; most marks are "lost" through a failure to be ambitious, interesting, or perceptive. Categories such as mechanics, on the other hand, can be a very different story. What do you think happens when you make the same spelling or grammatical error many times throughout the same paper? Some professors may deduct marks only for the first few instances of an error, then let you off the hook for the other ten times you misspelled an author's name or had a run-on sentence. Other professors, however, may keep on deducting marks. Ouch!

APPENDIX B

MORE ON CITATION

As we mentioned in Chapter 5, the purpose of citation is to ensure that the texts you refer to are recoverable by the reader. This is not only important to shore up your arguments (and poor citation most assuredly is a means to a worse mark), but it is also vital to ensure that you are not plagiarizing!

As you learned in Chapters 1 and 5, at a basic level, only the following information is needed to locate a source:

- who

- what

- where

- when

In other words, in all referencing styles, we need to know the author of the work, the title of the specific work you are referencing, where it was published, and the date of publication. For in-text citations that refer to a specific idea or argument expressed in a work or that contain a direct quote, we also need to know the page number(s).

This appendix gives you examples from Modern Language Association (MLA) style,[1] used for much of the humanities, and American Psychological Association (APA) style,[2] used for much of the sciences and social sciences. Each of these is further divided into in-text citations and citation lists (a.k.a. Bibliography, Works Cited, or References).

A QUICK NOTE ON INTEGRATING SOURCES

There are several ways to go about referencing other people's work in your essay, and each of these has advantages and disadvantages. The most important thing to remember, though,

REFERENCING: TWO CAUTIONARY TALES

I was once handed an essay that, except for the introduction and conclusion, contained *only* quotations from outside sources, with no writing whatsoever by the student. As you can imagine, it read horribly, and even though the student protested that she had (obviously) done a lot of research, I had to fail the paper on the grounds of unintelligibility and incoherence.

On the other side of the spectrum, I was once given a paper by a student who had obviously learned the formula "introduce a reference, give the reference, refer back to the reference," which she did in the following format: "I am going to cite this argument. Here is the citation of the argument. I just cited that argument." That one failed for triple redundancy!

is that referencing must be done as smoothly as possible: don't just dump a bunch of quotations into your work and hope that they are going to make it sound authoritative!

So how do you integrate sources well? The best student writing is going to appear seamless, meaning that the quotations are grammatically integrated into the larger sentences. Therefore, if you are going to use a quotation, you need to make sure that it isn't jarring—that it flows naturally from what you have previously said.

For example, let's say I am expected to use MLA format and want to use the following Bertrand Russell quote: "There is a special department of Hell for students of probability. In this department there are many typewriters and many monkeys. Every time that a monkey walks on a typewriter, it types by chance one of Shakespeare's sonnets."[3] First, the idea must certainly be embedded in the argument structure, as pointed out in previous chapters. So let's assume I am writing something about probability. Once I have ensured that the citation makes sense in the larger structure, I also need to make sure that it makes sense in the particular.

The easiest way of verifying that, given that my quotation comprises full sentences, is to use signal phrases. These are introductions such as "Russell argues that," "In the words of Bertrand Russell," "As Russell notes," "According to Russell," "In the words of Bertrand Russell," and other like phrases. If you do not use the name of the author in the signal phrase, you should include it in your in-text reference. For example, using MLA style, you would write:

> As one philosopher imagines, "There is a special department of Hell for students of probability. In this department there are many typewriters and many monkeys. Every time that a monkey walks on a typewriter, it types by chance one of Shakespeare's sonnets" (Russell 32).

If you are interested only in a single nominal group, such as Russell's expression "a special department of Hell for students of probability," then you must integrate the expression as a nominal group, which means that it will most likely be the grammatical object of your clause. It is grammatically incorrect to write the following: .

> As explained by Russell, "a special department of Hell for students of probability" (32).

This is technically a sentence fragment. Instead, you will want to make sure you include both a subject and a verb.

> Russell envisions "a special department of Hell for students of probability" (32).

One of the most effective ways of using references, though, is to simply paraphrase. Putting the arguments of experts into your own words and properly citing the source is an excellent way to lend authority to your own arguments: it proves that you have read and understood what you have read to the point that you can acknowledge it simply and personally. In the case of the above, you might write:

> Some metaphysicians imagine a special sort of everlasting punishment for statisticians, where every time a monkey walks across a keyboard, the output is a Shakespearean sonnet (Russell 32).

More on Citation **169**

MLA IN-TEXT CITATION

If your professor wants you to use MLA style, you are expected to ensure that all quotations include the author and the page number. You can do this either by using signal phrases with the author's name followed by the page number(s) in parentheses, or by including the author's name in parentheses after the quotation, as shown in the example above. Three things to keep in mind are that the date is not stressed in-text, there is no punctuation between the author and the page number, and there is no use of "p," "pp," or "pg" before the page numbers. Use a shortened form of the title when there is no author, or if you have multiple works by the same author. For works with multiple authors, if there are three or fewer, list them all; if there are four or more, give just the first author, followed by the abbreviation "et al."

EXAMPLES

Some studies suggest monkeys are capable of making their own beer ("Training Primate Brewers" 44).

Despite his own earlier findings (Watson, "Monkeys and Beer" 12), Watson later states that "amateurs should never give alcohol to simians" ("When Monkeys Go Bad" 92).

On the other hand, researchers have found beer to be a powerful motivator with civets (Irwin, Jovanovic-Krstic, and Barker 122).

One warning is clear, though: "Never get an ape drunk if he is bigger than you" (Barker et al. 4).

Finally, if you want to cite something that is actually a quote by another author, indicate that in-text. For example:

Irwin argues that "sober monkeys are a man's best friend" (qtd. in Watson 156).

Make sure you list both works in your bibliography. Or better yet, find the source text!

MLA CITATION LIST

Books

Single Author

The basic information is ordered as follows:

> Last name, First name. Title of Book. Publication city: Publisher name, Year of publication. Medium.
> Martin, Jim. *English Text: System and Structure.* Amsterdam: John Benjamins, 1992. Print.

Multiple Authors

If there are two or three authors, list them. If there are more than three, you may give just the first author and then use the short form "et al." Note that with several authors, only the first author has his or her name inverted (last name, first name) and the remaining authors are in regular order (first name then last name).

> Halliday, Michael, and Christian Matthiessen. *An Introduction to Functional Grammar,* 3rd ed. London: Arnold, 2004. Print.
> MacKinnon, Katherine, et al. *Primates in Perspective.* 2nd ed. Oxford: Oxford UP, 2010. Print.

Translated Work

The translator is included (first name, then last name) after the author and title.

> Aristotle. *The Art of Rhetoric.* Trans. Hugh C. Lawson-Tancred. London: Penguin, 1991. Print.

Edited Volume

If there is no primary author (as in a collection of essays), then the editor or editors are listed in that position.

> Ciochon, Russell, and Richard Nesbitt, eds. *The Primate Anthology: Essays on Primate Behavior, Ecology and Conservation from Natural History.* Upper Saddle River, NJ: Prentice-Hall, 1997. Print.

If there is an editor who has put together a text by a primary author, the author comes first, and the editor(s) comes after the title, with their names in standard format.

> Crawford, Isabella Valency. *Winona: Or, the Foster-Sisters*. Eds. Len Early and Michael Peterman. Peterborough, ON: Broadview, 2007. Print.

Chapter in a Book or Essay in a Collection

This is treated in essentially the same way as a journal article (see below) plus an edited volume. Note that the page numbers appear at the end.

> Rose, David. "Metafunctional Profile of the Grammar of Pitjantjatjara." *Language Typology: A Functional Perspective*. Eds. Alice Caffarel, Jim Martin, and Christian Matthiessen. Amsterdam: John Benjamins, 2004, 479-536. Print.

No Author

If there is no author available, the book is listed by its title.

> *Oxford English Dictionary*. Oxford: Oxford UP, 1989. Print.

Corporate Author or Government Publication

Since most of these works do not have a listed author, you simply incorporate the organization as the author.

> Canada. Government Office of Tourism. *Resources for Tourism, Hospitality, Recreation*. Ottawa: The Office of Tourism, 1979. Print.

Periodicals

Scholarly Journal Articles

This is an important one to remember, as you will be citing lots of these in your academic essays. You need the writer, the name of the article and journal, the volume and issue numbers, year of publication, and pages, in the following format:

Last name, First name. "Article Title." *Title of Periodical* Volume.Issue (Year): [page–page]. Medium.

Halliday, Michael. "On the Grammar of Pain." *Functions of Language* 5.1 (1998): 1–32. Print.

Magazine Articles

These are quite similar to journal articles, except that they deal with day (if weekly or bi-weekly) and month instead of volume and issue.

Brown, Chip. "The King Herself." *National Geographic* Apr. 2009: 88–111. Print.

Newspaper Articles

These are treated the same as magazines, but have different pagination (you need the section and the page):

Campion-Smith, Bruce. "Coalition Monkey Continues to Dog Harper." *Toronto Star* 30 Mar. 2011: A1. Print.

Electronic Sources

MLA no longer requires the use of URLs (web addresses) in the bibliography, but sometimes your professor will. If you include URLs, it is standard practice to include the URL in angled brackets, like so < >.

The information is basically the same as for print sources, but of course many online sources lack page numbers, or obvious publishing dates, or even publishers (which may bring into question their use in an academic essay!). The standard abbreviations are n.pag. (no page numbers), n.d. (no date), and n.p. (no publishing information).

Whole Website

If you can find an author or editor for the site, list that first; otherwise just list the name of the site, version number, institution (or publisher), date of creation, medium, date of access.

Greatapetrust.org. Trilix, 2002. Web. 4 Apr. 2011.

Individual Web Page or Article

These are essentially the same as the whole website, but with a title added in for the page:

> "Panbanisha." *Greatapetrust.org*. Trilix, 2002. Web. 4 Apr. 2011.

Images

These are cited using the artist, name of the work, the date of creation, and where it is housed. If it is electronic, you also need to indicate the website and the date of access.

Example of a physical image:

> Degas, Edgar. *Little Dancer, Aged Fourteen*. Circa 1880. Museu de Arte de São Paulo, São Paulo.

Example of the image appearing in a book:

> Degas, Edgar. *Little Dancer, Aged Fourteen*. Circa 1880. Museu de Arte de São Paulo, São Paulo. *Degas and the Little Dancer*. Richard Kendall. New Haven, CT: Yale UP, 1998. Cover. Print.

Example of the image on a website:

> Degas, Edgar. *Little Dancer, Aged Fourteen*. Circa 1880. Museu de Arte de São Paulo, São Paulo. *Museu de Arte de São Paulo*. Web. 4 Apr. 2011.

Online Journals

These are treated the same as print journals, except that the medium is "Web." If there is no pagination, you indicate this with "n. pag."

Digital Object Identifiers (DOI)

A DOI is a permanent link to an electronic article. They are typically used on web publications so that people can click on a citation to access an article. An example of a DOI is:

> Fring, A. and Manojlovic, N., "G2-Calogero-Moser Lax operators from reduction," Journal of Nonlinear Mathematical Physics, 13 (2006), 467-478. doi: 10.2991/jnmp.2006.13.4.1.

E-mail

This reference uses the author of the e-mail, the subject line, the person it was sent to, when it was sent, and the medium.

> Watson, Bruce. "Re: Citation Examples." Message to Derek Irwin. 2 Apr. 2011. E-mail.

Lectures

Give the lecturer's name, with a title if you have it, the name of the meeting and the location, the date, and a descriptor.

> Jovanovic-Krstic, Viktoria. ES1011 Composition. *Highly-effective writing strategies.* University of Toronto. 18 Jan. 2011. Lecture notes.

Audiovisual Media

Television Programs

Depending on whether the program is recorded or not, there is a slight difference in the medium. If it is a TV program on DVD, indicate that; if it is live, use the label "television" and include when and on what station it was broadcast. You can also include information on director (dir.), writer (writ.), performers (perf.), or producer (prod.) should you choose.

> "Episode #1.1." *The Joe Schmo Show.* Dirs. Danny Salles and Sean Travis. Agoura, CA: Spike TV. 2 Sep. 2003. Television.
>
> "Episode #1.1." *The Joe Schmo Show: Season One Uncensored!* Perf. Matt Kennedy Gould. Agoura, CA: Spike TV, 2003. DVD.

Movies

As with TV, there is a difference in citation format between whether the movie was viewed in a theatre (medium is Film) or recorded (medium is DVD). In either case, you need the name of the film, the director, the distributor, and the year, followed by the medium. You can also include writers (writ.) and performers (perf.) if relevant.

> *Twelve Monkeys*. Dir. Terry Gilliam. Perf. Bruce Willis and Brad Pitt. Universal Pictures, 1995. Film.

Music Recordings

Simply list artist, title, distributor, and date, followed by medium (CD, MP3, Audiocassette).

> N.W.A. *Straight Outta Compton*. Ruthless, 1988. CD.

APA IN-TEXT CITATION

The most important information in APA style is author, then date. The date follows the author's name, in parentheses. If there is no signal phrase, the author's name and date appear in the parentheses together. If you are going to directly cite a work, you need to include the page number, using either "p." for one page, or "pp. x–y" for multiple pages. If there are two authors, separate parenthetical references with an ampersand (&). The first mention of a work with multiple authors should mention them all, and subsequent mentions can make use of "et al."

For indirect references, include the author of the primary source in the signal phrase and the secondary source in parentheses.

Examples

> Irwin (2011) argues that we should befriend the lower primates, but not as drinking companions.

> According to Irwin (2011), "sober monkeys are a man's best friend" (p. 36).

> One contentious researcher claims that "sober monkeys are a man's best friend" (Irwin, 2011, p. 36).

> Irwin and Watson (2011) present many reasons to deny monkeys alcohol.

It has been found generally unwise, and often dangerous, to bribe monkeys with gin (Irwin & Watson, 2011).

Research has shown that intoxicated monkeys are unpredictable (Irwin, Jovanovic-Krstic, Watson & Watson, 2011).The same research has discovered several ways in which monkeys are actually more intelligent than their caregivers (Irwin et al., 2011).

Irwin argues that "many monkeys are in fact better companions than humans" (as cited in Watson, 2011, p. 156).

APA CITATION LIST
Books
Single Author
The basic format of the information for APA is as follows:

Last name, First initial(s). (Year). *Title of book*. Publication city: Publisher name.

Note that, unlike with MLA, authors are referred to by their last name and initials rather than their full name; the book title takes minimal capping; and the medium is not required.

Martin, J. (1992). *English text: System and structure*. Amsterdam: John Benjamins.

Multiple Authors
List all authors, with the final two separated by an ampersand. All names are inverted and are separated by commas.

Halliday, M. A. K., & Matthiessen, C. M. I. M. (2004). *An introduction to functional grammar* (3rd ed.). London, England: Arnold.

MacKinnon, K., Bearder, S., Stumpf, R. Campbell, C., & Fuentes, A. (2010). *Primates in perspective* (2nd ed.). Oxford: Oxford University Press.

Translated Work

The translator is included (first initials then last name) after the author and title. The initial date is that of the translation, and the original date is included in parentheses.

> Aristotle. (1991). *The art of rhetoric.* (H.C. Lawson-Tancred, Trans.). London, England: Penguin. (Original work published 350 BCE).

Edited Volume

If there is no primary author (as in a collection of essays), then the editor or editors are listed in that position.

> Ciochon, R., & Richard N. (Eds). (1997). *The primate anthology: Essays on primate behavior, ecology and conservation from natural history.* Upper Saddle River, NJ: Prentice-Hall.

If there is an editor who has put together a text by a primary author, the author comes first, and the editor(s) after the title, first initial then last name, followed by (Ed.).

> Crawford, I. V. (2007). *Winona: Or, the Foster-sisters.* L. Early & M. Peterman, (Eds.). Peterborough, ON: Broadview Press.

Chapter in a Book or Essay in a Collection

This is done in essentially the same way as a journal article (see below) plus an edited volume; there are no quotation marks around the chapter title. Note also that the page numbers appear before the publisher information, with the abbreviation "pp."

> Rose, D. (2004). Metafunctional profile of the grammar of Pitjantjatjara. In A. Caffarel, J. R. Martin, & C. M. I. M Matthiessen (Eds.). *Language typology: A functional perspective* (pp. 479–536). Amsterdam, Netherlands: John Benjamins.

No Author

If there is no author available, the book is listed by its title.

Oxford English dictionary. (1989). Oxford, England: Oxford University Press.

Corporate Author or Government Publication

The organization is the author, and the other information is in the same format as usual.

Canada Government Office of Tourism. (1979). *Resources for tourism, hospitality, recreation.* Ottawa: The Office of Tourism.

Periodicals

Scholarly Journal Articles

As with MLA, you need the writer, the name of the article and journal, the volume and issue numbers, year of publication, and pages. For periodicals, there is no use of the "pp." abbreviation. The format is the following:

Last name, Initial(s). (Year). Article title. *Periodical Name, Volume*(Issue), [page–page].
Halliday, M. A. K. (1998). On the grammar of pain. *Functions of Language, 5*(1), 1–32.

Magazine Articles

Brown, C. (2009, April). The king herself. *National Geographic, 215,* 88–111.

Newspaper Articles

These do include the abbreviation "p." or "pp."

Campion-Smith, B. (2011, March 30). Coalition monkey continues to dog Harper. *Toronto Star,* p. A1.

Electronic Sources

APA uses the indication "Retrieved from" before a URL. If you can find a Digital Object Identifier (DOI) number, you should include it. Thus, if you access a journal article electronically, you need to include this information.

Any missing information is indicated with "n.pag." (no page numbers), "n.d." (no date), and "n.p." (no publishing information).

Whole Website

These are generally not referenced in APA—refer to particular pages or articles on websites instead.

Individual Web Page or Article

Include as much information as possible. Note that it is much better to cite articles from academic journals than Web page information.

> Great Ape Trust. (2011). *Panbanisha*. Retrieved from http://www.greatapetrust.org/about-the-trust/meet-our-apes/panbanisha.
>
> Savage-Rumbaugh, S. (2011). Human language—Human consciousness. *On the human: A project of the National Humanities Center*. Retrieved from http://onthehuman.org/2011/01/human-language-human-consciousness/.

Images

In APA style, images usually comprise graphs or other objects. These are cited using the researching organization and date, followed by a description. If it is electronic, you also need to indicate the website.

> Max Planck Institute, Department of Primatology. (2008). [Map indicating bonobo range in Salonga National Park, D.R. Congo, November 27, 2008]. *Bonobo species research page*, G. Hohmann. Retrieved from http://www.eva.mpg.de/primat/files/bonobo.htm.

Online Journals

These are treated the same as print journals, except you need to include the URL or DOI, and if there is no pagination, you indicate it with "n. pag."

> Hershkovitz, P. (1984). Taxonomy of squirrel monkeys genus *Saimiri* (Cebidae, platyrrhini): A preliminary report with description of a hitherto unknown form. *American Journal of Primatology* 7(2), 155–210. doi: 10.1002/ajp.1350070212.

E-mail

E-mail correspondence is not listed in APA references; you cite them in-text, with author, date, and "personal communication":

> (B. Watson, personal communication, April 2, 2011).

Audiovisual Media
Television Programs

These are divided into entire series or individual episodes, which are indicated in brackets. A single episode concentrates on the writer, while a series is listed under the producer.

> Rheese, R. (Producer). (2003). *The Joe Schmo Show*. [Television series]. Agoura, CA: Spike TV.

> Moore, J. H., Reese, R., & Wernick, P. (Writers) & Salles, D. (Director). (September 3, 2003). Episode #1.1. In Rheese, R. (Producer). (2003). *The Joe Schmo Show*. [Television series]. Agoura, CA: Spike TV.

Movies

If possible, list producer and director in the author position, followed by their title in parentheses. The medium is in square brackets, and the country and studio are listed last.

Cavallo, R. (Producer), & Gilliam, T. (Director). (1995). *Twelve Monkeys*. [Motion picture]. United States: Universal Pictures.

Music Recordings

The sequence is songwriter, date of copyright, artist information in square brackets, title, and medium in brackets. Location and label come last.

Wright, E. E., Jackson, O., & Patterson, L. (1988). Straight Outta Compton. [Recorded by N.W.A.]. On *Straight Outta Compton* [CD]. Los Angeles, CA: Ruthless Records.

NOTES

1. *MLA Handbook for Writers of Research Papers*. 7th ed. New York: MLA, 2009. Print.

2. *Publication Manual of the American Psychological Association*. 6th ed. Washington, D.C.: APA, 2009. Print.

3. Russell, Bertrand. "The Metaphysician's Nightmare." *Nightmares of Eminent Persons and Other Stories*. London: The Bodley Head, 1954. 32. Print.

INDEX

' (apostrophes), 120, 124
— (dashes), 5
- (hyphens), 5
; (semicolons), 28, 49, 144–145

A

acronyms, 77
active verbs, 70
ad hominem attacks (personal attacks), 85–86
additive connections, 59
adjectives, 131–133
adverbs, 59–60, 131–133
adversative connections, 59
alternation patterns, 68–69
ambiguity, 34–36
American Psychological Association (APA) in-text citation, 176–182
   audiovisual media
      movies, 181–182
      music recordings, 182
      television programs, 181
   books
      chapters in book, or essays in collection, 178
      corporate author or government publication, 179
      edited volume, 178
      multiple authors, 177
      no author, 178–179
      single author, 177
      translated work, 178
   electronic sources
      individual web page or article, 180
      overview, 179–180
      whole website, 180
   e-mail, 181

   images, 180
   online journals, 181
   overview, 111–112
   periodicals
      magazine articles, 179
      newspaper articles, 179
      scholarly journal articles, 179
analogies, opening with, 37–38
analysis category, Bloom's Taxonomy, 79
Analysis marking category, 162
analytical reading, 6–8
analyzing, defined, 4
anaphora, 134
anastrophe, 134
anecdotes, opening with, 37–38
Answers the Question marking category, 163
antistrophe, 134–135
antonymy, 58
APA. *See* American Psychological Association (APA) in-text citation
apostrophes ('), 120, 124
application category, Bloom's Taxonomy, 79
appositive connections, 59
arguable claims, 98
arguing, defined, 4
Argument marking category, 161–162
arguments, 75–89
   critical approach, 75–76
   errors in, 82–89
   objective analysis
      applying, 80–81
      moving from subjective to, 77–80
   organizing around
      backing, 100–102
      claims, 97–99, 104–107

(arguments, organizing around,
  continued)
    data, 96–97
    overview, 95–96
    qualifiers, 102–104
    warrants, 99–100
  overview, 76–77
Aristotle, 82
assigned reading
  overview, 5–6
  "so what?" and "seems to be
  about" models, 6–8
asyndeton, 134
audience
  reader interest, generating,
  35–36
  writing for, 8–9, 93–94
audiovisual media, citation of
  movies
    APA, 181–182
    MLA, 175–176
  music recordings
    APA, 182
    MLA, 176
  television programs
    APA, 181
    MLA, 175
authors, citation of
  corporate
    APA, 179
    MLA, 172
  multiple
    APA, 177
    MLA, 171
  none
    APA, 178–179
    MLA, 172
  overview, 17
  single
    APA, 177
    MLA, 171

B

background paragraphs, 115
backing, Toulmin model, 100–102
Begging the Question, 84

Black and White World
  arguments, 85
block patterns, 69
Bloom's Taxonomy, 78–80
body paragraphs, 53–73. *See also*
  organization
  cohesion and coherence in
    overview, 58
    textual cohesion, 60
    through connection, 59–60
    through repetition, 58–59
  concluding sentences, 72–73
  defining, 53
  developing
    overview, 61
    using definitions, 61–62
    using explanation, 62–63
    using qualification, 63
  examples
    appropriate, 55–56
    elaboration, extension,
    and enhancement
    through, 57–58
    overview, 56–57
  integrating, 113–114
  order of, 114–115
  organizing
    first drafts, 63–64
    overview, 63
    patterns of development,
    66–69
    structure, 64–66
  roles of, 54
  spicing up, 69–71
  topic sentences
    overview, 54–55
    supporting with
    examples, 55–56
    writing effective, 55–56
books, citation of
  chapters in book, or essays in
  collection
    APA, 178
    MLA, 172
  corporate author
    APA, 179
    MLA, 172

edited volume
    APA, 178
    MLA, 171–172
government publication
    APA, 179
    MLA, 172
multiple authors
    APA, 177
    MLA, 171
no author
    APA, 178–179
    MLA, 172
single author
    APA, 177
    MLA, 171
translated work
    APA, 178
    MLA, 171

C

calls to action, 123
capitalization, 151
category, defining by, 61–62
causal connections, 60
cause-and-effect paragraphs, 65–66
cheating. *See* plagiarism
Chicago Manual of Style (CMS)
    in-text citation, 111–112
Citation (Documentation) marking
    category, 163
citations, 167–182
    APA, 111–112, 176–182
        audiovisual media,
            181–182
        books, 177–179
        electronic sources,
            179–180
        e-mail, 181
        images, 180
        online journals, 181
        periodicals, 179
    avoiding plagiarism, 17-20
    CMS, 111–112
    examples of poor, 168
    integrating sources, 167–169
    MLA, 111–112, 170–176

audiovisual media,
    175–176
books, 171–172
Digital Object Identifiers,
    174–175
electronic sources,
    173–174
e-mail, 175
images, 174
lectures, 175
online journals, 174
periodicals, 172–173
overview, 110–111, 167
claims, Toulmin model
    beginning arguments with,
        104–106
    evaluating, 106–107
    identifying, 105–106
    overview, 97–99
    relationship of qualifiers and
        rebuttals to, 103
clauses
    combining
        overview, 142–143
        through coordination,
            143–145
        through subordination,
            145–146
    as message
        Hyper-theme, 153
        Macro-theme, 153–154
        overview, 152
        Theme, 152–153
    most important ideas in main,
        49–50
    overview, 137–138
clichés, 147–148
climatic order, 67
climax, 135
Clinton, Bill, 87
closing arguments (final stand
    statements), 121–122
CMS (*Chicago Manual of Style*)
    in-text citation, 111–112
coherence
    in body paragraphs, 58–60
    in introductions, 33–35

cohesiveness (cohesion)
  in introductions, 33–35
  reader interest and, 35
  textual, 60
  through connection, 59–60
  through repetition, 58–59
comma splices, 143, 146
common knowledge versus learned
  information, 16
comparative connections, 60
comparisons in body paragraphs,
  64–65
complementary introductions and
  conclusions, 120–121
complex sentences, 72, 145
complexity, incorporating, without
  sacrificing clarity, 48–49
compound sentences, 72, 143–145
comprehension category, Bloom's
  Taxonomy, 78–79
Comprehension of Material
  marking category, 162
concessive connections, 60
concluding sentences, 72–73
conclusions, 117–125
  to avoid
    repeated thesis, 119
    sudden endings,
      118–119
    surprise endings, 119–
      120
  driving point home
    applying idea to bigger
      context, 124–125
    calls to action, 123
    overview, 122–123
    suggesting further
      research, 124
  as frame for body, 92
  key elements of successful
    culmination, 122
    final stand, 121–122
    overview, 120–121
  Organization marking
    category, 160
  overview, 117–118, 125
conditional connections, 60

conjunctive adverbs or phrases,
  59–60
connection, cohesion through,
  59–60
contrasts in body paragraphs, 65
coordination, combining clauses
  through, 143–145
corrective connections, 59
correlation versus causality, 85
critical reading, 6–8
culmination, 122

D

dangling participles, 150–151
dashes (—), 5
data, Toulmin model, 96–97
deductive approach (logical
  approach), 40, 67–69
defining
  by category, 61–62
  by negation, 61
  by synonym, 61
definitions
  developing body paragraphs
    using, 61–62
  opening with, 38–40
dependent clauses, 48
Digital Object Identifiers (DOI),
  174–175
discussion section. See body
  paragraphs; organization
dismissive connections, 59
Documentation (Citation) marking
  category, 163
DOI (Digital Object Identifiers),
  174–175

E

edited volumes, citation of
  APA in-text citation, 178
  MLA in-text citation,
    171–172
effect, cause and, 65–66
Einstein, Albert, 92
elaboration through examples,
  57–58

electronic sources, citation of
  documenting, 18
  e-mail
    APA, 181
    MLA, 175
  individual web page or article
    APA, 180
    MLA, 174
  online journals
    APA, 181
    MLA, 174
  overview
    APA, 179–180
    MLA, 173
  whole website
    APA, 180
    MLA, 173
e-mail, citation of
  APA, 181
  MLA, 175
encyclopedias, 39
enhancement through examples,
  57–58
ethos, 82
evaluation category, Bloom's
  Taxonomy, 79–80
examining, defined, 4
examples
  appropriate, 55–56
  elaboration, extension, and
    enhancement through,
    57–58
  overview, 56–57
explanation, developing body
  paragraphs using, 62–63
extension through examples,
  57–58

F

fallacies, 82–89
false analogies, 85–86
falsifiable claims, 98
FANBOYS mnemonic, 144
faulty modification, 131–132
fewer versus *less*, 21
final stand statements, 121–122

first drafts
  of body paragraphs,
    63–64
  containing more topics than
    final draft, 34, 36
  importance of, 663–664
  purpose of, 43–44
first person pronouns, avoiding,
  75–77, 148–149
focus, generating in introduction,
  35–36
formal outlines, using sentences to
  create, 21–23
Formatting and Style Guide, online
  writing lab (OWL) at Purdue
  University, 16
framing
  body with introduction and
    conclusion, 92
  as strategy, 46–47
funnel (logical approach), 40,
  67–69

G

Given–New relationship, 60
government publications, citation of
  APA, 179
  MLA, 172
grading. *See* marking schemes
grammar, 137–154
  a lot, 12
  active verbs, 70
  "anyways", 130
  apostrophes, 120, 124
  to be, 128
  beginning sentences with
    this, 93
  capitalization, 151
  clauses
    combining, 142–146
    as message, 152–154
    overview, 137–138
  clichés, 147–148
  combining multiple forms of
    punctuation, 100
  dangling participles, 150–151

(grammar, *continued*)
    dashes, 5
    fewer versus *less*, 21
    first person, 148–149
    first words of sentences, 108
    hyphens, 5
    it's versus *its*, 97
    numbering, 149–150
    passive voice, 150
    possessive pronouns, 124
    reflexive pronouns, 114
    repetition, 147
    second person, 149
    semicolons, 28
    simple sentences
        nominal groups and
            pronoun reference,
            139–140
        overview, 138–139
        parallel construction,
            141–142
        subject–verb agreement,
            142
    split infinitives, 122
    style versus, 133
    tense shifts, 148
    than versus *then*, 62
    transition phrases, 4
    transitive verbs, 128
    verb agreement with subject
        head, 56
    who versus *whom*, 81
    wordiness, 147
    your versus *you're*, 104

H

Halliday, M.A.K., 57–60
Heckman, Grant, 14
Hyper-theme, 153
hyphens (-), 5
hyponymy, 59

I

Illustration and Proof marking
   category, 162–163
illustrations, 62–63

images, citation of
    APA, 180
    MLA, 174
imitation journals, 156–157
imprecise pronouns, 140
independent clauses, 49
inductive order, 67
information collection. *See* research
instructions, understanding, 3–5
integration
    of paragraphs, 113–114
    of sources, 167–169
    of transition terms or phrases,
       59
interpretative process, 6–8
introductions, 31–40
    cohesiveness and coherence,
       33–35
    focus, generating, 35–36
    as frame for body, 92
    keeping hard copy while
       writing, 115
    Organization marking
       category, 159
    overview, 31
    reader interest, generating,
       35–36
    strategies for
        analogies, 37–38
        anecdotes, 37–38
        definitions, 38–40
        logical approach, 40
        overly general statements,
            37
        overview, 36–37
        procedural openings, 38
        quotations, 40
        startling statements, 37
        summary of, 41
    writing last, 33
inverted pyramid (logical
   approach), 40, 67–69
it's versus *its*, 97

K

Kane, Thomas, 55
key sentences, 69

knowledge category, Bloom's
Taxonomy, 78
Known–New Contract, 60

L

layered reasoning, 97
learned information versus
common knowledge, 16
lectures, MLA in-text citation of, 175
less versus *fewer*, 21
library, information collection at,
17–19
logical approach (deductive
approach), 40, 67–69
logical fallacies, 82–89
logical relationships, 48
logos, 82–83

M

Macro-theme, 153–154
magazine articles, citation of
APA, 179
MLA, 173
marking schemes, 159–165
categories
Analysis, 162
Answers the Question, 163
Argument, 161–162
Citation
(Documentation), 163
Comprehension of
Material, 162
how professors use,
163–165
Illustration and Proof,
162–163
Organization, 159–161
Sentence and Paragraph
Mechanics, 161
Style, 161
overview, 159
translation of number grades
to letter grades, 164–165
Matthiessen, C.M.I.M., 57–60
metaphors, 62
metonymy, 59

Modern Language Association
(MLA) in-text citation,
111–112, 168–176
audiovisual media
movies, 175–176
music recordings, 176
television programs, 175
books
chapters in book, or
essays in collection, 172
corporate author
or government
publication, 172
edited volumes, 171–172
multiple authors, 171
no author, 172
single author, 171
translated works, 171
citation, 112
Digital Object Identifiers,
174–175
electronic sources
individual web page or
article, 174
overview, 173
whole website, 173
e-mail, 175
images, 174
lectures, 175
online journals, 174
periodicals
magazine articles, 173
newspaper articles, 173
scholarly journal articles,
172–173
movies, citation of
APA, 181–182
MLA, 175–176
music recordings, citation of
APA, 182
MLA, 176

N

negation, defining by, 61
newspaper articles, citation of
APA, 179
MLA, 173

Newton, Isaac, 103
nominal groups and pronoun
reference, 139–140
numbers
    personal pronouns and,
        140–142
    spelling out, 149–150

O

objective analysis
    applying, 80–81
    moving from subjective to,
        77–80
online journals, citation of
    APA, 181
    MLA, 174
online sources, citation of. *See*
  electronic sources, citation of
order of paragraphs, 114–115
organization, 91–116. *See also*
  citations
    of body paragraphs
        first drafts, 63–64
        overview, 63
        patterns of development,
          66–69
        structure, 64–66
    integration, 113–114
    introduction and conclusion as
      frame, 92
    linking paragraphs to purpose,
      91
    order, 114–115
    research
        as organizing device,
          109
        relevance of material,
          112–113
    Toulmin model, 95–104
        backing, 100–102
        claims, 97–99, 104–107
        data, 96–97
        overview, 95–96,
          107–108
        qualifiers, 102–104
        rebuttals, 102–104

    topic sentences,
      108–109
    warrants, 99–100
  traditional approach
    overview, 92–93
    university-level essays,
      93–95
Organization marking category,
  159–161
outlines
    formal, 21–23
    hierarchical structure of,
      25–28
    overview, 20–21
    process, 23–28
    purpose statements
      overview, 10
      writing, 11–12
    role of, 9–10
    scratch, 21
    writing each point as full
      sentence, 115–116
overly general statements, 37

P

page limits, importance of,
  4–5
paragraphs. *See also* body
  paragraphs; organization
    background, 115
    breaking in middle of,
      115–116
    integration of, 113–114
    length of, 57
    linking to purpose, 91
    order of, 114–115
    Organization marking
      category, 160–161
    structure of, 53
parallel construction,
  141–142
parallel sentences, 69
paraphrasing, 169
passive voice, 150, 152
pathos, 82
periodic sentences, 69–70

periodicals, citation of
    magazine articles
        APA, 179
        MLA, 173
    newspaper articles
        APA, 179
        MLA, 173
    scholarly journal articles
        APA, 179
        MLA, 172–173
personal attacks (ad hominem
    attacks), 85–86
plagiarism
    avoiding, 16–20
    common knowledge versus
        learned information, 16
    defining, 14–16
    example of, 15
    intentional, 14–15
    overview, 13–14
    unintentional, 15–16
polysyndeton, 134
possessive pronouns, 124
pre-writing process, 1–29
    assigned reading
        overview, 5–6
        "so what?" and "seems to
           be about" models, 6–8
    audience, writing for, 8–9
    benefits of, 1–2
    instructions, understanding, 3–5
    outlines
        formal, 21–23
        overview, 20–21
        process, 23–28
        purpose statements,
           10–12
        role of, 9–10
        scratch, 21
    overview, 1–2
    research
        citations, 17–20
        at library, 17–19
        overview, 13
        plagiarism, 13–16
    thinking about essay and
        topic, 2–3

procedural openings, 38
pronoun reference issues, 139–140
pronouns
    first person, avoiding, 75–77,
        148–149
    imprecise, 140
    possessive, 124
    reflexive, 114
    second person, 149
proper adjectives, 151
punctuation
    apostrophes, 120, 124
    combining multiple forms of,
        100
    dashes, 5
    hyphens, 5
    semicolons, 28, 49, 144–145
purpose statements
    overview, 10
    writing, 11–12
Pyrcz, Heather, 55

Q

qualification, developing body
    paragraphs using, 63
qualifiers, Toulmin model, 102–104
quotations, opening with, 40

R

rebuttals, Toulmin model,
    102–104
"red herring" technique, 88
redundancy, 147
reflexive pronouns, 114
reiteration, 58
repeated thesis, 119
repetition
    cohesion through, 58–59
    poor form, 147
research. *See also* citations
    bibliographic information,
        17–18
    at library, 17–19
    online, 18
    as organizing device, 109
    overview, 13

(research, *continued*)
   plagiarism
      common knowledge
         versus learned
         information, 16
      defining, 14–16
      overview, 13–14
   quoting versus summarizing,
      18
   relevance of material,
      112–113
   suggesting further, in
      conclusion, 124
   taking notes from, 17–19
   tips for, 20
respective connections, 60
revision process, 127–135
   adverbs and adjectives,
      131–133
   considerations during,
      128–130
   editing versus, 127–128
   eliminating clutter, 130–131
   overview, 32, 127–128
   rhetorical devices and, 133–135
rhetoric, 82
rhetorical devices and revision
   process, 133–135
Rosenwasser, David, 6
run-on sentences, 143, 146

S

scholarly journal articles,
   citation of
      APA, 179
      MLA, 172–173
scratch outlines, 21
second person, 149
secondary sources. *See* citations;
   research
"seems to be about" model,
   6–8
semantic arguments, 84, 87
semicolons (;), 28, 49, 144–145
Sentence and Paragraph Mechanics
   marking category, 161

sentence fragments, 139, 145
sentence outlines, 21–23
sentences
   beginning with *this*, 93
   complex, 72, 145
   compound, 72, 143–145
   concluding, 72–73
   first words of, 108
   key, 69
   most common errors, 138
   parallel, 69
   periodic, 69–70
   run-on, 143, 146
   simple
      nominal groups and
         pronoun reference,
         139–140
      overview, 138–139
      parallel construction,
         141–142
      subject–verb agreement,
         142
   topic
      overview, 54–55
      supporting with
         examples, 55–56
      value as organizing
         device, 108–109
      writing effective, 55–56
   using to create formal outlines,
      21–23
   varying length of, 69
similes, 62
simple sentences
   nominal groups and pronoun
      reference, 139–140
   overview, 138–139
   parallel construction, 141–142
   subject–verb agreement, 142
slippery slope arguments, 87–88
"so what?" model, 6–8
sob stories, 88
specific versus general wording,
   133
split infinitives, 122
startling statements, 37
Stephen, Jill, 6

Straw Man arguments, 88
Style marking category, 161
subjective analysis, 77–80
subject–verb agreement, 142
subordinating conjunctions, 48
subordination, combining clauses
   through, 145–146
sudden endings, 118–119
summative connections, 59
surprise endings, 119–120
synonym, defining by, 61
synonymy, 58
synthesis category, Bloom's
   Taxonomy, 79

T

taking sides, 45
television programs, citation of
   APA, 181
   MLA, 175
temporal connections, 60
tense shifts, 148
texting shorthand, 110
textual cohesion, 60
than versus *then*, 62
Theme, 152–153
theories, 46
thesis statements
   fixing, 47–50
   focus, 42
   getting from topic to thesis
      framing as strategy,
         46–47
      overview, 44–46
   hypothesis, 50–51
   importance of, 42–44
   overview, 10, 40–42
   purpose statements, 11–12
   questions regarding, 43–44
topic outlines, 21–23
topic sentences
   overview, 54–55
   supporting with examples,
      55–56
   value as organizing device,
      108–109

   writing effective, 55–56
topical theses, 105
Toulmin model, 95–104
   backing, 100–102
   claims
      beginning arguments
         with, 104–106
      evaluating, 106–107
      overview, 97–99
   data, 96–97
   overview, 95–96, 107–108
   qualifiers, 102–104
   rebuttals, 102–104
   topic sentences, 108–109
   warrants, 99–100
transition phrases, 4
transitive verbs, 128
translated works, citation of
   APA in-text citation, 178
   MLA in-text citation, 171
two-part theses, 49

V

vague references, 140
van Dijk, Margaret, 55
variative connections, 60
verbs
   active, 70
   agreement with subject head,
      56
   shifting tense, 148
   subject–verb agreement, 142
   tense shifts, 148
   transitive, 128
verificative connections, 59

W

warrants, Toulmin model
   backing versus, 100–102
   overview, 99–100
   relationship of qualifiers and
      rebuttals to, 103
web pages or articles, citation of
   APA, 180
   MLA, 174

websites, citation of
    APA, 180
    MLA, 173
who versus *whom*, 81
Whose Burden of Proof?
    arguments, 88–89

Wikipedia, 39
word limits, importance of, 4–5
wordiness, 130–131, 147

Y

your versus *you're*, 104